STONYHURST SCRIPTURE MANUALS

GENERAL EDITOR: PHILIP CARAMAN, S.J.

THE GOSPEL ACCORDING TO SAINT JOHN

THE
GOSPEL ACCORDING
TO SAINT JOHN

With an Introduction and Commentary

by

C. C. MARTINDALE, S.J.

THE NEWMAN PRESS

Westminster Maryland

This edition first published 1957

PRINTED IN GREAT BRITAIN BY WESTERN PRINTING
SERVICES LTD BRISTOL. IMPRIMI POTEST J. D. BOYLE,
S.J., PRAEP. PROV. ANGL. SOC. JESU. NIHIL OBSTAT
JOANNES M. T. BARTON, S.T.D., L.S.S., CENSOR
DEPUTATUS. IMPRIMATUR C. MORRAGH BERNARD,
VIC. GEN., WESTMONASTERII, DIE 17 JULII, 1956

EDITORIAL NOTE

STONYHURST Scripture Manuals fill many of the needs satisfied fifty years ago by the Manuals of Father Sydney Smith, S.J., of *The Month* staff. These earlier works are now out of print and, in any case, unsuited to present needs.

The commentary and notes are the work of Father C. C. Martindale, who has a long-standing reputation for Biblical scholarship. In order to pass on the benefit of his knowledge to the beginner, he has worked throughout in collaboration with members of the Stonyhurst staff who have many years of experience in teaching Scripture.

Any individual or group engaged in studying the New Testament will find in this and successive volumes the means of deepening their knowledge of the life and Person of Christ, and so of coming to a truer and more intimate understanding of Him.

PHILIP CARAMAN, S.J.

Volat avis sine meta
Quo nec vates nec propheta
Evolavit altius.
Tam implenda quam impleta
Numquam vidit tot secreta
Purus homo purius.

GENERAL INTRODUCTION

THIS series is intended for the use of schools, especially for those who enter for public examination, and therefore the version called the 'Douay' has throughout been quoted, despite the imperfections whether of the English translation or the Latin original. The notes have been kept as short as possible: we have not made use of devotional comments or applications, nor, save by exception, strictly theological ones. On the other hand, we have tried to include what might throw light on the conditions in which our Lord lived and spoke. It would be impossible to catalogue the authorities that we have used: happily we can now refer to the *Catholic Commentary on Holy Scripture* (1953): besides, we have the Westminster Version with its notes, and the books by the late Fr Hugh Pope, O.P., and the monumental volumes produced by the late Fr M.-J. Lagrange, O.P., our debt to whom we never can repay.

A practical difficulty remains. The books on the Synoptists are produced separately, so that there cannot but be many repetitions unless teacher or pupil have all three at hand and are ready to refer constantly from one to the other. Pupils, at least, are not likely to do this: therefore the repetitions cannot be avoided, though the difficulty of 'harmonization' will not always be surmounted. But the *Commentary* alluded to above should give the teacher all he needs to know.

The inclusion of a certain number of Greek words should not deter boys or schools who do not take that language. They are always given with the (Douay) English; and are quoted because the English often does not and sometimes cannot render the full flavour of the Greek. Besides, some

Greek words may be used chiefly, or only, by the author in question, and 'characterize' him, and he ought to be given his chance of 'coming to life', even though the English equivalents may be, at best, very imperfect.

The text used is the 'Douay' version, published at Rheims (1582) and modified by Bishop Challoner in 1746. The 'Vulgate', of which this is a translation, was itself translated from the Greek by St Jerome, who died A.D. 420; when alluded to here, the abbreviation 'Vg' is used. Naturally, we have kept our eyes chiefly on the use of this series in schools, and accordingly have not alluded to many hypotheses about the 'Fourth Gospel' or to references which would have their proper place in a work of adult scholarship, but which would overload these pages. May we add that we hope that these notes will be of service also to teachers? It is unlikely that students at school will be left to read them entirely by themselves. Teaching is co-operative; something may remain obscure to the student unless he be helped by the teacher; and the teacher constantly finds that he is himself forced to learn simply because he has to explain. Nor are we content with maintaining some existing 'standard', but wish to be steadily raising it.

INTRODUCTION TO SAINT JOHN

I PRELIMINARY

It has often been denied, in modern times, that the Apostle John, son of Zebedee (Mark 1: 19), wrote this document, and doubted whether we can rely on it as an historical account of our Lord Jesus Christ. Hebrews, when writing historical narratives, did not sign their names to them; but prophets did name themselves at the head of their prophecy. So, if St John (as we hold) wrote both his historical Gospel and the Apocalypse, it was normal that he should name himself in the latter, but not in the former. We ask, then, first, what outside evidence there is for the Johannine authorship. The historian Eusebius of Caesarea says (about A.D. 320): 'Of the undoubted writings of this Apostle, surely his gospel which is read by all the churches under Heaven must be the first to receive acknowledgement.' He also quotes Origen (d. 254) who held that John was the last of the Evangelists to write his 'gospel', and says, in effect, that none could truly fathom it unless he, like John, had leaned upon the breast of Jesus and had received Mary for his mother: and Origen's teacher, Clement of Alexandria (d. about 215) says that John, 'last of all', considered that the other evangelists had sufficiently set forth the 'material' (τὰ σωματικά) facts of our Lord's life and, urged by his friends and moved by the Holy Spirit, composed a 'spiritual gospel' (πνευματικὸν εὐαγγέλιον). And Tertullian (about 200) appeals to all four evangelists by name against the heretic Marcion. But passing to the Asiatic world, Theophilus, bishop of Antioch (Syria), about 179, mentions John as author of our gospel and counts him among the 'inspired' (πνευματόφοροι): Polycrates, bishop of

Ephesus (about 180), is quoted by Eusebius as appealing to the authority of the Apostles Philip and John as justifying the Asiatic date for celebrating Easter, 'according to the gospel', and defines this John as being he who reclined upon the breast of our Lord. The most important witness is however Irenaeus who wrote his 'Against Heresies' between 175 and 189; born in Asia, bishop of Lyons, acquainted with Rome, he knew the Church from east to west: he had been taught by St Polycarp of Smyrna, himself a disciple of St John. He quotes some hundred verses from our gospel, often adding: 'as John, the disciple of the Lord, says . . .' And after speaking of the three Synoptists, he writes: 'Then John, the disciple of the Lord, who had indeed rested on his breast, himself too published a gospel when living at Ephesus in Asia.'

Some confusion is due to a statement of Papias, bishop of Hierapolis (about A.D. 130), quoted by Eusebius. He mentions Andrew, Peter, Philip, Thomas, James, John and Matthew as sources of his information and then mentions Aristion and 'the presbyter John'. Papias asked 'the elders' what the Apostles, John included, had said, and then adds Aristion (of whom nothing more is really known) and a 'presbyter John'. This John is either the Apostle, already named, or vanishes from view till Dionysius of Alexandria (264–5), who seems to have been the first to suggest that there were two Johns. He does this, not for historical reasons, but because he (and others) held that the Apostle could not have written the Apocalypse (and the reason for this was that they thought it contained a fantastic prophecy of a thousand years' earthly enjoyment for Christians before the Last Day). So, since they held firmly that the Apostle John wrote the Gospel, they said that it must have been the 'Presbyter John' who wrote the Apocalypse and indeed the Second and Third Epistles of 'St John'. In modern times the theory of the 'two Johns' has been revived, but on the whole abandoned; some non-Catholic writers grant that the Apostle *may* have written the Apocalypse, but not the Gospel, because, say they, the ex-fisherman John could not have thought out so developed and mystical a 'theology' as that of the Fourth Gospel. It is interesting that the existence of a family Ti. Claudius Aristion at Ephesus has been ascertained though its tombs cannot be shown to be Christian. See p. xvii for the argument that John could not have written the gospel bearing his name because he was martyred along with his brother James in A.D. 44 (Acts 12: 1–2).

II St John as Author

Can we derive any evidence as to authorship from the gospel itself? But first, what is known of the Apostle John otherwise than from the 'Fourth Gospel'? John and his brother James were sons of Zebedee (Mark 1: 19) who hired men to help in his trade of fisherman in the Lake of Galilee. He and James were called by our Lord after Andrew and Simon had been called, and they were nicknamed 'Sons of the Thunderbolt', 'Thunderbolt men', because of their impetuous temperament (Mark 3: 17)—it was they who asked that the village which had refused admittance to our Lord should be blasted with fire from heaven (Luke 9: 54); and they who ambitiously asked to be the two most important men in the coming Kingdom (Matt. 20: 20). It was John who wished our Lord to stop a Jewish exorcist from using His name (Mark 9: 37–38). He alone with Peter and James witnessed the raising to life of the daughter of Jairus, the Transfiguration and the Agony in Gethsemani. In the Synoptists, Peter is always named first, John, third or fourth; but in the Acts, the order is: Peter, John, James, Andrew. Peter and John kept close together; they worked the miracle at the gate of the Temple (Acts 3: 1): were before the Sanhedrin together (4: 13) and visited Samaria (8: 14). James was martyred in 42 or 44; John is not said to have been arrested along with Peter (12: 3) and was one of the 'pillars' of the Church in Jerusalem referred to by Paul (Gal. 2: 9).

But we have the right to identify 'the disciple whom Jesus

loved', so often mentioned in the 'Fourth Gospel', with St John who, were it not he, would not be mentioned in that document at all, which has rightly been called unthinkable. He was surely the companion of Andrew mentioned in John 1: 40, and since, like Andrew, he had been a disciple of the Baptist, we see at once that he is likely to have had an insight into the mind of the Baptist himself and of Simon, Andrew's brother. The author now seems to disappear till 13: 23, when the 'disciple whom Jesus loved' is found lying next to our Lord at the supper-table, so that by leaning back his head was close to our Lord and he could ask in a whisper (urged to do so by Simon) who the traitor was: in 18: 15 it was surely he who entered the high-priest's house and afterwards brought Peter in (Acts 4: 13 need create no difficulty, though there he seems unknown to the authorities: on the night of the Thursday there was a crowd, and oriental crowds are always noisy; and while he appealed to his acquaintance with the high-priest in order to get himself allowed in, once *in* he may well have kept himself in the background and not have been noticed). He stood on Calvary and to him our Lord entrusted His Mother (19: 26); he witnessed the piercing of the side and insists that his witness is true (19: 35); see the note on that verse: it is he who runs with Peter to the tomb (20: 2); who recognizes our Lord, back in Galilee, and speaks at once to Peter (21: 7); and it is of the destiny only of these two that our Lord speaks in 21: 20 ff.

It does not seem very likely that the gospel was written first in Aramaic and then translated, like St Matthew's: on the other hand, it is proved that John sometimes thinks like a Palestinian even when writing in Greek; and when he uses, instinctively, an Aramaic or Hebrew word, he translates it for his Greek-speaking hearers—e.g. Messias, Kephas, Rabbi, Rabboni, Golgotha. More important is the fact that he is quite familiar with places and times—e.g. 'the Pool of Bethsaida by the Sheep Gate having five porticos' (see on 5: 2): now some writers have actually argued from the fact that John says: 'there *is* a Pool etc.' that the gospel was written quite early in John's life, because, by the time it had always been thought to have been written, Jerusalem and the Pool must have long ago been destroyed. This is to make no allowance for John's visualizing past events so clearly that they seem actually present—besides, the 'five porticos' had provided a puzzle till excavation showed that the Probatic Pool had a portico on all four sides and a sort of bridge-arcade across the middle. In his vivid account of our Lord's discourse with the Samaritan woman at the well, he recalls that in her excitement due to her talk with Him she ran back to the town *leaving behind her* the very pitcher she had come to draw water with (4: 28); and in her talk she speaks so naturally of Mount Gerizim, without naming it, as 'this' mountain, close to the foot of which the well was. It is John who mentions that the five loaves (6: 9) were barley-loaves and that there was much grass at that place; that the men came to arrest our Lord 'with lanterns and torches' (18: 3), and that the man whose ear Peter cut off was called Malchus (18: 10); and he often mentions the very hour when an event took place, though such details add nothing to the substance of the story, but do add to its vividness. On the other hand, he remembers that Mary Magdalen, coming from the empty tomb to the Apostles, cried: 'They have taken away the Lord . . . and *we* know not where they have laid Him', not observing that he had not mentioned that other women had been with her—he was not there himself, and he remembered only what *he* had been concerned in (20: 2). Vivid as St Mark's narrative is, still it can but echo St Peter's memories, and contains nothing so brilliantly vivid as St John's description of the healing of the man born blind (c. 9): one might almost say that this is an example of St John's restrained sense of humour, or at least irony. Still, all this could not *prove* that St John was an eye-witness, though it makes it far easier to suppose that he was than that he was not; he *might* have been an extremely skilful 'artist' in literature, except that if that were all, he would be unique. No ancient writer composed what we should call 'historical romances', getting all the details archaeologically right—even the prefaces to Plato's Dialogues are brief pictorial 'settings' for the argument that follows.

We may add that in St John's time parchment was expensive, and writing with a stylus on papyrus not much easier than writing with a knitting-needle upon cloth: so we are not surprised if documents like the Gospels became widely known —not because everyone had a copy, but because they were read to the 'community'; thus a writer like St Ignatius of Antioch could *allude* to the evangelists (and John in particular, whose record must have circulated at first chiefly in Asia Minor) without actually quoting him as author of the familiar words. But it would be impossible to make a list of all such allusions. The important point is that John underlines the fact that he was, precisely, an eye-witness.

III CHARACTER OF THE GOSPEL

'Witness' is a word that occurs so often in St John's Gospel that we could almost call his record 'a Book of Witnesses'. He appeals to Moses and the Prophets, to the Baptist, to the Miracles (which are, for him, essentially 'signs' pointing beyond themselves), to our Lord Himself as witnessing to the truth of what John writes about Him. But in 1: 14, he says: 'The Word was made flesh, and we beheld His glory', and even if 'we beheld' suggests that others beside himself contemplated our Lord during His earthly life, he certainly includes himself. The plural by no means indicates that the 'gospel' was written by a group of Christians, or expressed their ideas in a way not normal among their fellow-believers. In 1 John 1: 1 ff., nothing is clearer than that the author (who is certainly the author also of the Gospel) is appealing to his personal experience: 'That which we have heard, that which we have seen with our eyes, that which we have watched and our hands have handled . . . yes! the Life was made manifest, and we have seen, and we are bearing witness, and we are announcing to you . . . that which we have seen and have heard we are announcing to you too, in order that you too may have fellowship with us.' John passes quite naturally from singular to plural when referring to himself: Epistle I, 1: 4; 'we write', and 'I write' 2: 1; and 'I wrote' 2: 21. One has to judge by the context: thus in John 21: 24, 'This is the disciple who is bearing witness about these things and wrote these things, and we know that his witness is true'; 'we know' (οἴδαμεν), seems clearly to refer to the circle of St John's friends (not, we think, to others of the original Twelve. Who knows if any were then surviving?); but, it is an attestation to St John's authorship: while after the piercing of our Lord's side (19: 35), 'He who has seen has given witness—and his witness is truthful, and *He* knows that he is telling the truth, so that you too may believe', this is, we feel, *not* a note by some 'editor' but is written by St John himself about himself: and if it seems startling that he should use only the emphatic pronoun 'He' (ἐκεῖνος) when invoking God (or our Lord) to go guarantee for his truthfulness, see 1 John 1: 6; 3: 3, 5, 7, 16; 4: 17.

Now the whole of this appeal to 'witness', and to his own eye-witness, would have been downright dishonest as well as useless, had John been writing mere allegory, speculative theology, symbolized here and there by scenes from an idealized 'life' of Christ. He is writing history; but, what kind of history? Not exactly the same sort as the Synoptists wrote (still less is John just filling up gaps left by them); they are, so to say, the servants of their material; they do not choose their goal but keep close to the authoritative oral tradition (and if St Matthew and St Luke add matter of their own, it is the same *sort* of matter—some more information about our Lord's childhood; some more parables or sayings): true, they are not mere machines; each has his personal style; Matthew wrote with his eye chiefly on the Jews; St Luke, on non-Palestinians: but St John selects and arranges his material so as to drive home

a sublime doctrine about Christ—Christ the source of that
'Eternal Life' which is to be given also to men so far as they
can assimilate it—'Jesus, then, did many other "signs" in the
presence of His disciples which are not written in this book;
but *these have* been written that you may believe that Jesus is
the Christ, the Son of God, and that believing, you may have
Life in His name' (20: 30, 31).

The language in which St John clothes his message is
certainly unlike that of the Synoptists.[1]

But for some the difficulty is this—St John himself writes,
and seems to make our Lord, or the Baptist, speak, in just the
same *sort* of words and phrasing. Can we judge, therefore,
whether we really are told what each speaker said, or has St
John 'recast' his account so that it is St John to whom we are
listening throughout, and the discourses, at any rate, are really
his invention? Now it is true that early MSS. did not use
inverted commas, brackets or as a rule 'stops' like colons etc.,
so that it is not always easy to see where the narrative, or the
quotation, is broken off, or even, sometimes, where a sentence
ends. We must, then, remember that St John was definitely
a witness, *and* that he was not a stenographer. He was not
even present at the talks of our Lord with Nicodemus (c.3) or
the Samaritan woman (c.4). And many of His discourses
lasted a long time, yet St John may fill only a page or two with
his reports of them. Moreover, the Synoptists often, and St
John himself (2: 22), insist that the disciples frequently failed

---

[1] It has been argued that the Greek of the Gospel is so different from that of
the Apocalypse that the same man could not have written both documents.
This book is not about the Apocalypse, so, without going into details, we may
say: (1) it is perverse to suppose that a man cannot write in quite different
styles, using different vocabularies, if he has reason for doing so. If we had
only St Thomas Aquinas's philosophical works, who would have guessed that
he could write his hymns? Or that St John of the Cross, had we only his
mystical poems, or only his ascetical treatises, could have written both?
(2) The Apocalypse belongs to a definite *kind* of writing, as different as possible
from any other kind, and had its traditional laws of symbolism and diction.
(3) There are sufficient hints in the Greek of the Gospel and the Apocalypse to
suggest that both were written by the same man: but we are not dealing with
the latter here, and need say no more.

to grasp the full meaning of what our Lord said when He said it: only later did they grasp that meaning. And St John, after a long life spent meditating on those words, penetrated depth after depth in the divine message, and no fact remained mere fact, but was seen to be a 'sign' pointing to something much further than itself. We may, then, assume that St John, in his old age, remembered (as old men will) details of his youthful experiences more vividly than what had happened in middle-life, and *also*, appreciated their whole significance far better than he had as a young man. This does not disregard divine Inspiration which will have guided him to say only what was true and what God wished; but inspiration does not supersede the laws that govern the development of the human mind. In short, as Fr J. Lebreton wrote in his *Histoire du Dogme de la Ste. Trinité* (p. 377), 'The personal stamp is so strongly impressed upon John's whole work that the book seems woven of one piece throughout, prologue, narrative, discourses.... At times the interpretation and the discourse are so intimately united that it is hard to discern where Christ's speech ends and the Apostle's own reflections begin.... The revelation comes authentically from Jesus; but today it is across the soul of St John that we behold it.... Yet, though seen only across John's soul, it is Christ's self we see: He is not John's creation.'

As for St John's later life, little is known of it. We disregard the legend that he was killed along with his brother James by Herod Agrippa in A.D. 44, for which there is no real evidence at all. There is good evidence that he went to Ephesus, but probably not before Paul's final departure in 66-7: here his disciple Polycarp became a Christian in 69. Probably too it was under Domitian that he was exiled to the mines of the island Patmos where he wrote the Apocalypse, returning under Nerva (96-8), and writing his Gospel not long before his death. Much of his time will have been spent in caring for our Lady so long as she lived; a few stories show that his impetuous spirit had not died out—he refused so much as to stay in the same building as the heretic Cerinthus; yet he had no rest till he had converted a young robber; he liked to play, they relate, with a pet partridge; he almost tired his disciples with his Christ-like exhortation to love one another; it was they, probably, who helped him to put his Gospel into writing.

VERSIONS REFERRED TO

The Septuagint (LXX); the Greek version of the Old Testament (O.T.).

The Vulgate (Vg.); the Latin version of both O. and N. Testaments.

The Douay Version, made from the Vg. at Rheims and Douay, 1582–1610. This is the text used in this series.

The Authorized and Revised Versions (A.V. and R.V.) are those used in the Church of England and other denominations.

NOTE ON SCRIBES, PHARISEES, SADDUCEES

These names occur so often in the Gospels that it may be simplest to say once and for all what they stand for.

The Scribes. For the Jew, religion meant the 'Law', and the Law meant the rules for life written down, it was held, by Moses. The Scribes, though not priests, were more and more important as interpreters of the Law: true, they might not always agree—there were 'schools of thought' among them, some more rigid, some more lax. In point of fact, it was they who accumulated a mass of regulations which they claimed to be the proper way of applying the Law to actual circumstances. Such were the rules concerning the Sabbath, fasting, the washing of hands; clean or unclean foods, objects or persons. Thus an intolerable yoke was laid on the consciences of would-be law-abiding Jews.

The Pharisees, which means 'Separatists'—a name that may have been given to them at first as a mere nickname, like 'Christian' itself—numbered, it is thought, about 6,000, and plumed themselves on not being 'as other men are', even their fellow-Jews. They professed to obey all the rules laid down by the Scribes, and many of them made a public display of their observances. Hence, if they really did act up to their profession, they were apt to become intolerably proud; if they did not, they were hypocrites, and it is by no means only our Lord who called them so. They were inclined to be nationalists, and in fact (Josephus tells us: he lived from 37 to about A.D. 100) they refused to take an oath of allegiance to the Emperor Augustus or to King Herod the Great.

Their tragedy was, that while officially representing the ancestral religion, and insisting on the purity of its observances, they turned it into something quite beyond what the ordinary Jew, even pious, could practise.

The Sadducees claimed to derive their name from Zadok, the high-priest in the days of Solomon. It is certain that they adhered more or less closely to the heirs of the Maccabees who had developed a priest-king line. They were, on the whole, 'aristocrats', the Pharisees belonged more to the 'middle-class'. But they took second place in popular esteem, so impressive had the Pharisees made themselves: besides, it was known that the Sadducees were 'broad-minded', if not lax; they disbelieved in a spiritual world of angels, and in personal survival. They would have wished to be on good terms with the pagan governments of the day. It is clear how, in different ways, these three groups were bound to find themselves opposed to our Lord.[1]

[1] Many amusing and enlightening anecdotes about these people can be found in Dr J. P. Arendzen's *Prophets, Priests and Publicans*, although this book appeared so long ago as 1926.

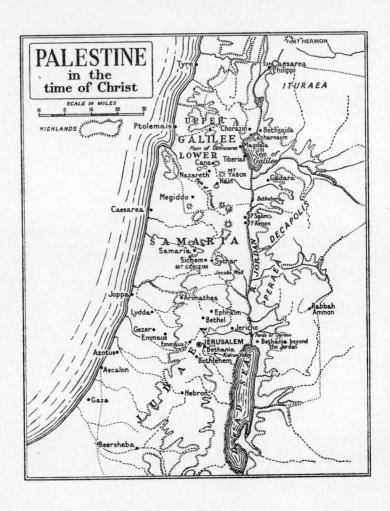

PALESTINE
in the
time of Christ

SCALE IN MILES
10   20   30

HIGHLANDS

MT HERMON

Tyre

Caesarea
Philippi

ITURAEA

Ptolemais

UPPER
GALILEE

Chorazin

Bethsaida
Capharnaum

Plain of Genesaret

Magdala

Sea of
Galilee

LOWER

Cana

Tiberias

Nazareth

MT
TABOR

Nain

Gadara

Megiddo

Bethebara

Caesarea

DECAPOLIS

?Salim
?Aenon

SAMARIA

Samaria

Sichem

MT GERIZIM

Sychar

Jacob's Well

R. JORDAN

PERAEA

Joppa

Arimathea

Lydda

Ephraim

Bethel

Gezer

Jericho

Rabbah
Ammon

Emmaus

Fords of Jordan

Emmaus

JERUSALEM

Bethania beyond
the Jordan

Azotus

Bethania

Kidron Valley

Bethlehem

Ascalon

DEAD SEA

JUDAEA

Hebron

Gaza

Beersheba

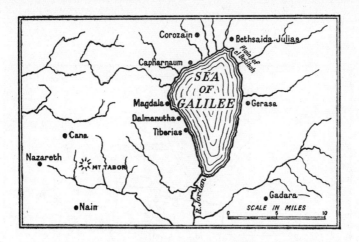

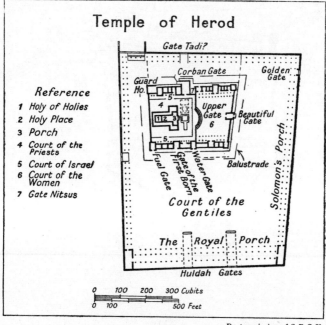

Temple of Herod

Gate Tadi?

Corban Gate

Golden Gate

Guard Ho.

Upper Gate

Beautiful Gate

Solomon's Porch

Balustrade

Fuel Gate

Gate of the First Born

Water Gate

Court of the Gentiles

The Royal Porch

Huldah Gates

Reference
1. Holy of Holies
2. Holy Place
3. Porch
4. Court of the Priests
5. Court of Israel
6. Court of the Women
7. Gate Nitsus

0   100   200   300 Cubits
0   100   500 Feet

By permission of S.P.C.K.

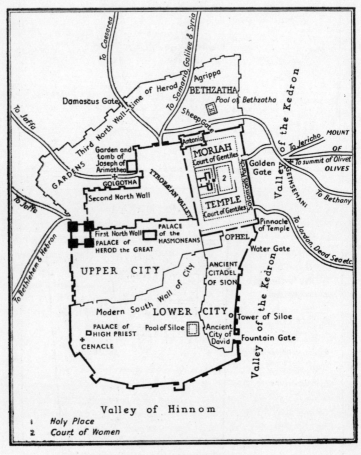

PLAN OF JERUSALEM

1   *Holy Place*
2   *Court of Women*

xxiv

SAINT JOHN

CHAPTER ONE

Prologue (i): 1–8

1. In the beginning was the Word: and the Word was with God: and the Word was God.
2. The same was in the beginning with God.
3. All things were made by him: and without him was made nothing that was made.

---

1. 'In the beginning the Word existed', or rather, 'was existing'. St John is certainly referring to Gen. 1: 1; but he does not mean that the Word began to exist when the created universe did; His existence is, as we should say, 'in eternity'.—'And the Word was with God': we have no preposition which will adequately render the Greek for 'with' here (or in 1 John 1: 2: 'the life which was with, πρός, the Father): nor indeed in any language can we adequately express the relationship of the Three Divine Persons in one God to one another. St John wishes to say that the Word is mysteriously other than Him who utters it; yet forthwith, lest we should be in any danger of thinking He was less than, or separated from God, he proceeds: 'and the Word *was* God'. We may make this human comparison—I can speak of 'my' idea: yet my idea is nothing else than myself thinking. See Note on p. 171.

2. St John recapitulates emphatically what he has said about the Word and God—'This Word, of whom I have said that He was God, and with God, existed from eternity with God.' He then passes to the relation of the Word to Creation.

3. 'All things came into being by means of Him, and without

4. In him was life: and the life was the light of men.
5. And the light shineth in darkness: and the darkness did not comprehend it.

Him nothing came into being that did come to be'; this is the Vulgate punctuation (since 1590 printers have made the comma into a full-stop): and an assertion followed by a denial of its opposite is not uncommon: cf. Isa. 39: 4: 'They saw all that was in my house; there was nothing I did not show them'; and Jer. 42: 4. St Paul says (1 Cor. 8: 6): 'One God, the Father, from whom (ἐξ οὗ) are all things . . . and one Lord, Jesus Christ, by means of whom (δι' οὗ) are all things'. Here too we could compare: 'I made my statue by means of the vivid idea I had in my mind': the *idea* is interior; hammer and chisel exterior. But *God* needs no outside agent to assist Him. The Old Testament too spoke of God creating by His Word and His Wisdom (cf. Prov. 8: 30): and again, St Paul, Heb. 1: 2.

4. 'In Him was Life, and the Life was the Light of men': this is according to the Vulgate punctuation. St John does not yet define what he means by 'Life' and by 'Light': all that he will have to say about 'Life' has its source in God's Word, and that Life does not remain enclosed in God's mind, but is a Light that shines forth and reaches man. We need not spend time over the meaning of these words if they are punctuated differently. For example, by putting a full stop after 'nothing' (οὐδὲ ἕν), we could proceed: 'That which has come to exist in Him, is life (i.e. alive)', to which it may be hard to attach an exact sense: or, 'That which has come to exist, in Him is life', i.e. finds its only true life in, by reason of its incorporation with, Him. But we do not think that John has the Incarnation, or Christ's 'Mystical Body', so far, directly in view. We think that he first asserts that save by means of the Word, nothing at all was created: then, that the Word is the source of all life; and then, that this life communicates itself to man's mind like Light.

6. There was a man sent from God, whose name was John.

7. This man came for a witness, to give testimony of the light, that all men might believe through him.

8. He was not the light, but was to give testimony of the light.

---

5. 'And the Light is shining in the darkness, and the darkness did not quench it': the Vulgate translates οὐ κατέλαβεν 'non comprehenderunt', meaning, presumably, 'did not understand it'. But we think it far more probable that the word means 'to lay hold of so as to conquer it, extinguish it'. John is thinking of mankind, not as it might have been (had there been no sin) but as it actually has been, hostile to the Light and resisting it, but unable to 'catch up with it' and quench it. All this will be made clearer as the Gospel proceeds.

6. 'There came a man . . .' Almost 'arrived', 'entered on the scene': ἐγένετο need not be written deliberately in contrast with 'there existed' (verse 1); still, the Baptist's created nature and arrival in time cannot but be contrasted with the eternal existence of the Word, rather as 'sent from' (παρά) God cannot but be contrasted with the Word's mysterious existence 'with' (πρός) God: and 'his *name* was John' is again in strongly contrasted parallel with 'The Word *was God*'. The Evangelist, who never mentions his own name, has no need to define this 'John' as 'the Baptist'; there was no one else who he could possibly be! Besides, he is at once defined by his role.

7. 'This man came for (or, as) a witness.' Here St John strikes a keynote to his gospel (cf. p. xiv): his aim is to make people believe in our Lord, and he will accumulate witnesses to the rightness of his claims about Him. 'That all men should believe by means of him': this does not mean only those who actually listened to the Baptist; soon enough, his voice would no more be heard; and others would be more 'official' witnesses than he: but his words go on echoing and we too value his unique witness, and it is a pity that the intense medieval devotion to the Baptist has died out.

8. 'Not that *he was* the Light'; the pronoun (ἐκεῖνος) is

3

Prologue (ii): 9–14

9. That was the true light, which enlighteneth every man that cometh into this world.

10. He was in the world: and the world was made by him: and the world knew him not.

11. He came unto his own: and his own received him not.

---

emphatic: we need not suppose that anyone, when St John wrote, was satisfied with the 'baptism of John' (cf. Acts: 19) and that the evangelist wishes to put the Baptist down to his proper position; but he does wish to place our Lord in *His* unique place.

9. The Light (of which St John has spoken in verse 4 and to which the Baptist bore witness) was the 'true', 'real' Light, compared with which the light given to our bodily eyes is hardly more than shadow; but should we construe 'coming into the world' with the light, or, with 'every man'? We prefer: 'That was the true Light, that shines on every man, making its way into the world.' But in what sense can the supernatural Light be said to be shining upon every man? We can but answer that God gives sufficient grace for salvation to every man without exception, and that all grace is granted owing to the merits of Jesus Christ. He is the fountain of Light that radiates all around itself. We do not think that

10. St John is referring exclusively and directly to the Incarnate Word before verse 10, when we hear definitely of opposition being given to the Word—He (for the pronouns are now masculine, agreeing with 'Word' (λόγος), not neuter, agreeing with Light (φῶς), came into the world which had been created through Him, but the world failed to recognize

11. Him; and to 'His own'—which must mean Palestine and the Jews—and they did not accept Him. But the rejection was not universal; some *did* receive Him, and to these He gave power to become children of God, to be more than they had been by merely natural birth, i.e. children of men, men and

4

12. But as many as received him, he gave them power to be made the sons of God, to them that believe in his name.

13. Who are born, not of blood, nor of the will of the flesh, nor of the will of man, but of God.

---

nothing more. But we ask: 'If a man "receives" Him, is he not forthwith a "child of God"? How then does he receive "power" to "become" a child of God?' We do not think that John was referring directly to Baptism here, though he will inevitably have had it 'at the back of his mind', simply because those who 'accepted' Christ always were baptized and knew that they would have to be. John defines what he means by 'receiving' our Lord: they who do so are those who 'believe in His Name': the moment they do so, they not only *can* become 'children of God', but actually become so, for St John means, by 'believing on His Name', no mere intellectual agreement that Jesus is the Son of God, but an act of will whereby the whole believer makes himself over to Him. The power to do this, and the will to do it, are alike the gift of God; they can be distinguished by our minds, but in the concrete are assumed to be simultaneous. The 'Name' really means the 'Person': the believer makes himself over, as a living person, to that Person who is Jesus Christ, the Son of God made man for us (cf. 1 John 5: 1, 5). Though this coming into existence of a 'child of God' demands a real activity

13. on man's part, St John now makes it absolutely plain that the essential gift is due to God's act and not at all to man's: 'these are born, not from blood, nor from fleshly desire nor the desire of a man, but from God': the point of the sentence as a whole is clear, even if the bearing of each word is not—St John insists that the becoming a 'child of God' is due to no physical origin, nor to human instinct, nor to the choice of a man, but comes from God. Many Greek Fathers (and the Latin translation of Irenaeus, but Tertullian alone among Latin writers) show that there was a tradition that this verse should be read: 'Who (i.e. He) was born' (ὅς for οἵ; and

14. And the Word was made flesh and dwelt among us (and we saw his glory, the glory as it were of the only begotten of the Father), full of grace and truth.

ἐγεννήθη for ἐγεννήθησαν): making the meaning to be that He in whose name men must believe came into being not from any human cause, but was, as the Church teaches, virgin-born. We may think it strange that St John insists so heavily on what the origin of the children of God is *not*; and, that he does not allude to the virgin-birth of our Lord. However, the 'new birth' of the child of God is precisely what he wants to emphasize as supernatural, as we see too in his First Epistle (2: 29; 3: 9; 4: 7; 5: 4,18. And cf. the Third Epistle, 3–8). It is unnecessary to spend time speculating about *why* the false version arose: it is possible that St John's authentic words suggested to some readers that the 'children of God' somehow had no human parentage at all, and that they changed the words into what they thought made better sense.

14. Many have said that no sentence more tremendous than this one has been written. The term *Logos* reappears, and for the last time in this Gospel. We recall all that St John has said of it. Then follows that declaration which, quite strictly, outpasses human language. For 'flesh' (σάρξ) means 'man' (not flesh as contrasted with soul); the expression serves to emphasize the extreme opposite—the farther side of a gulf that could not, we might have thought, be bridged. Nor have we an adequate word to serve St John's meaning: 'became', 'was made', both could suggest that the Logos was *turned into* flesh: in fact, the Mystery of the Incarnation cannot be properly expressed in words taken from human experience. The 'and' (καί), with which the sentence begins, sums up and accounts for all that has been said about those who 'received' Him—'Yes! the Word became Man, and spread His tent amongst us': John used this word, σκηνοῦν, twice in the Apocalypse (7: 15; 21: 3) which (being so Hebrew in

6

colouring) makes it the more certain that he here has in mind the Shekinah, which has the same consonants and is not unlike in sound. The Shekinah ('dwelling') was the 'cloud' which manifested the presence of God, e.g. in the Tabernacle (Ex. 33: 7–11) and the Temple (3 Kings, 8: 10–11); later it was used instead of the Name itself of God. Some think that 'amongst us' means in Palestine, and those in particular who *did* 'recognize' Jesus as Son of God; in which case 'we beheld' refers to these: others think that John means simply that God dwelt among men as Man, and that mortal eyes beheld His glory. Whether John speaks in the name of a group of eye-witnesses, or of himself in the plural (as writers often do), it remains that he at least includes himself among eye-witnesses; and the 'glory' may have been that which was manifested by the miracles, in the Transfiguration, or that eradiation of the Divinity which, though not seen with the eyes, none the less made itself felt in close personal association (cf. on Luke 9: 32). 'As' ($\dot{\omega}s$) does not mean 'comparable with' what a Sole-Begotten Son of God would have, but, more nearly, 'the glory proper to a Sole-Begotten . . .': St John prefers the word 'sole-begotten' ($\mu o\nu o\gamma\epsilon\nu\eta s$) to 'first-begotten' ($\pi\rho\omega\tau o\gamma\epsilon\nu\eta s$) which suggests the possibility of other Sons existing. In the text here used, 'we beheld . . . Father' is a parenthesis, so that 'full' ($\pi\lambda\eta\rho\eta s$) would be nominative agreeing with the Logos: but $\pi\lambda\eta\rho\eta s$ could also be regarded as an undeclinable word and belong to 'Sole-Begotten': 'grace and truth' come together in Ex. 34: 6, but rather in the sense of 'favour' and 'fidelity': St John means more than that: the Word Incarnate is the very source of Goodness and of Truth.

It may prove best to read the Prologue rather rapidly, and return to it when the rest of the Gospel has been studied. It is like a great Gateway, with the King's escutcheon emblazoned above it; we pass through into the outer courts of the castle, without examining in detail all that is on the shield. St John has stated the leading ideas of his Gospel without dwelling on them—Life, Light, Truth: he has expressed the contrast to

15. John beareth witness of him and crieth out, saying: This was he of whom I spoke: He that shall come after me is preferred before me: because he was before me.

16. And of his fulness we all have received: and grace for grace.

17. For the law was given by Moses: grace and truth came by Jesus Christ.

Light, i.e. Darkness, only implying those of Death and the Lie; nor has he yet mentioned a subordinate idea (depending really on Light), i.e. Walking as opposed to 'wandering', going nowhere in particular (save indeed to disaster). He has emphasized the idea of Witness; and indeed it has been suggested that he wrote his Prologue after writing the rest, in which case verse 15 would be added as a sort of transition: the Baptist reappears, briefly, before becoming a central figure, but not so as to make John forget the glories of which he has sung—in fact, verse 16 joins easily straight on to 14.

15. The English is an antiquated translation. 'He who came after me'—St John the Baptist was born before Jesus, and appeared on the scene before Him: yet Jesus has passed ahead of him: the real reason being, because 'He existed before me' and is on a higher plane than I. The words for 'before' are ἐμπροσθέν and πρῶτος: the former signifies that Jesus has come second but has passed on ahead: the latter is frequently used for πρότερος; John's own mind does not forget that the Word was 'in the Beginning'—is eternal.

16. John continues what he was saying in 14.
The word 'fulness' (πλήρωμα) is not used in the special sense proper to St Paul, but means that *all* 'grace' has its source in Jesus Christ, and from that source 'all we' (St John surely looks out at least to all those who read and believe him)

17. have received 'favour after favour'. We may feel that any allusion to Moses is somewhat intrusive: still, St John was a Jew, and the Law had played a great part in his life: he makes a double distinction—the Law was 'given', instituted, by

8

18. No man hath seen God at any time: the only begotten Son who is in the bosom of the Father, he hath declared him.

The Transition from the Baptist to Jesus (i): 19–22

19. And this is the testimony of John, when the Jews sent from Jerusalem priests and Levites to him, to ask him: Who art thou?
20. And he confessed and did not deny: and he confessed: I am not the Christ.

Moses; Grace 'came to exist' through Jesus Christ: the Law implied an obligation and a prohibition; Grace is a free gift.

18. God Himself remains invisible; even Moses (despite e.g. Ex. 33: 11) did not see Him face to face: 'A Sole-Begotten Son, who exists in the breast of the Father, *He* made the Revelation.' Important MSS. have: 'A Sole-Begotten God'; but this expression would be unique in John, whereas 3: 16, 18 and 1 John 4: 9 make (to our mind) 'Son' the more probable reading. He hath declared (i.e. proclaimed)—('explained' is not a very good translation, when the object is God)—is followed by no accusative case. Yet, since St John has just said that no one has *seen* God, what else, save God, can be the matter of 'manifestation', or revelation? In short, Jesus *is* the Word, the 'expression' of God: it is *in Him* that we are to look for, and that we shall find, God. 'In the bosom' (εἰς τὸν κόλπον): the εἰς is hard to translate: cf. πρός in verse 1. The Son is with (πρός) the Father, looks towards Him and then towards us, and 'speaks the Father forth': cf. 14: 16. St John is concerned here only with the Baptist's witness to Jesus, and omits everything else, even the Baptism (save by indirect allusion in 5: 32).

19. The 'Jews' are already almost symbolical of the opposition: 'priests and Levites' are naturally associated, as the leaders and 'subordinate companions'.

20. The Baptist answers the unspoken question: he 'acknowledges' that he is not the Christ. '*I* am not the Christ.'

21. And they asked him: What then? Art thou Elias? And he said: I am not. Art thou the prophet? And he answered: No.

22. They said therefore unto him: Who art thou, that we may give an answer to them that sent us? What sayest thou of thyself?

The Transition from the Baptist to Jesus (ii): 23–28

23. He said: *I am the voice of one crying in the wilderness, make straight the way of the Lord*, as said the prophet Isaias.

24. And they that were sent were of the Pharisees.

25. And they asked him and said to him: Why then dost thou baptize, if thou be not Christ, nor Elias, nor the prophet?

26. John answered them, saying: I baptize with water: but there hath stood one in the midst of you, whom you know not.

27. The same is he that shall come after me, who is preferred before me: the latchet of whose shoe I am not worthy to loose.

---

21. They insist—'Who then? Elias?' He had created such a sensation that they felt he might at least be the Messias's predecessor, for they expected Elias in person. (The story of John's birth can have aroused only a local surprise, and during his long eclipse it must have been quite forgotten.)

22. Moses (Dt. 18: 15) had predicted 'a prophet' who would be listened to. Some identified this with the Messias (cf. 6: 14); others, not (7: 40). The Baptist, ever more curtly, says 'No': they insist on *some* answer.

23. St John quotes only the first part of the well-known reply.

24. 'And there were sent some from among the Pharisees': more aggressively they ask by what right, then, does John baptize?

26, 27. He answers elliptically: 'I baptize with water . . . there is one standing (actually) amongst you whom *you* do not know:' implying: 'but *I* do'. 'Who is preferred before me' may be due to the words in verse 30; and cf. the expression 'stronger than I' in Matthew and Mark: here the Baptist certainly says that He who comes after him is none the less his

28. These things were done in Bethania, beyond the Jordan, where John was baptizing.

The Transition from the Baptist to Jesus (iii): 29–34

29. The next day, John saw Jesus coming to him; and he saith: Behold the Lamb of God. Behold him who taketh away the sin of the world.

30. This is he of whom I said: After me there cometh a man, who is preferred before me: because he was before me.

31. And I knew him not: but that he may be made manifest in Israel, therefore am I come baptizing with water.

---

superior—he is not worthy so much as to loose (so Mark and Luke: Matthew has 'lift', i.e. carry) the thong of His sandals.

28. This Bethany is unknown. It was on the other side of Jordan, but not the place where Jesus had previously Himself been baptized, nor of course the Bethany upon Mount Olivet.

29. So far, John had said that his Successor was present but unseen. Now he points to Him: 'There He is!' And he adds, 'The Lamb of God, who takes away the sin of the world!' John had had his vision of the Dove, as he will say in a moment: also he had intimately felt the innocence of Jesus (Matthew 3: 14)—an innocence such that it does away with the evil that the world in its long history had accumulated. A lamb was sacrificed morning and evening in the Temple; and the Paschal Lamb was offered, but recalled the escape of Israel from Egypt, not the remission of their sins. In Acts 8: 32, Philip refers to Isaias 53: 7, a Messianic passage in which God's Servant is compared to a lamb silent before its shearers. The figure of the Messias, pure and purifying, is in keeping with what the Baptist has said of Him cleansing His threshing-floor.

30. 'This is the man of whom I said that He came after me, but has come to be before me—for He *existed* before me.' This affirmation of the pre-existence of our Lord is so astonishing that the Baptist has to make it clear how he knows of it.

31. 'And I myself did not know Him; but it was that He might be revealed to Israel that I came, I who baptized with water . . .

32. And John gave testimony, saying: I saw the Spirit coming down, as a dove from heaven; and he remained upon him.

33. And I knew him not; but he who sent me to baptize with water said to me: He upon whom thou shalt see the Spirit descending and remaining upon him, he it is that baptizeth with the Holy Ghost.

34. And I saw: and I gave testimony that this is the Son of God.

The Transition from the Baptist to Jesus (iv): *The Calling of Andrew and Peter:* 35–42

35. The next day again John stood and two of his disciples.

32–34. (And he bore witness)—'I watched the Spirit descending from heaven . . . and He remained upon Him: yes, even I did not know Him, but He who sent me to baptize with water, *He* said to me: "On whomsoever you shall see the Spirit descending and remaining on Him, that is He who baptizes with the Holy Ghost." And I did see, and have been bearing witness that this is the "Son of God"' (perhaps 'the Chosen One of God' should be read). We think it possible—so tremendous are these affirmations—that the Baptist spoke them to a small group only, especially as our Lord was to take long before he allowed His Messiahship to be proclaimed. The outpouring of the Holy Ghost upon the Messias was fully prophesied by Isaias (11: 1; 42: 1; 61: 2): also, we shall see that the word for 'world' ($\kappa \acute{o} \sigma \mu o s$), and the word for 'to remain' ($\mu \acute{e} \nu \epsilon \iota \nu$) are favourite ones of the Evangelist, and the former would be unparalleled on the Baptist's lips: so perhaps the 'witness' given by him is partly cast in the Evangelist's style.

35. The picture is clear: John is standing with his disciples; Jesus is passing by; the Baptist looks hard at him ($\grave{\epsilon} \mu \beta \lambda \acute{\epsilon} \psi a s$), points to Him and repeats the words that may 'yesterday' have startled, but today spur on to action. Two of his disciples follow Jesus though at a distance. One is Andrew; the other must be John, who will not name himself but allows himself to be inferred (cf. 13: 23; 20: 2, etc.). He is not called 'the

36. And beholding Jesus walking, he saith: Behold the Lamb of God.

37. And the two disciples heard him speak: and they followed Jesus.

38. And Jesus turning and seeing them following him, saith to them: What seek you? Who said to him: Rabbi (which is to say, being interpreted, Master), where dwellest thou?

39. He said to them: Come and see. They came and saw where he abode: and they stayed with him that day. Now it was about the tenth hour.

40. And Andrew, the brother of Simon Peter, was one of the two who had heard of John and followed him.

41. He findeth first his brother Simon and saith to him: We have found the Messias, which is, being interpreted, the Christ.

42. And he brought him to Jesus. And Jesus looking upon him, said: Thou art Simon the son of Jona. Thou shalt be called Cephas, which is interpreted Peter.

---

disciple whom Jesus loved', for after all, this was their first meeting. The account is quite simple: yet John, looking back at the event after very many years and having acquired his own habit of mind, can hardly but have felt a deeper meaning in words like 'follow', 'seek', and 'dwell' ($\check{\epsilon}\mu\epsilon\iota\nu\alpha\varsigma$: as we should say: 'Where are you staying?').

39. Our Lord bids them welcome, and John remembers that it was four o'clock and that this first unforgettable interview lasted the rest of that day.

40. Presumably Andrew fetched Simon the same day (for which there was plenty of time), unless we regard St John's 'next day' as meaning no more than 'next', or 'afterwards', like St Matthew's 'then' and St Mark's 'immediately'. Andrew had anyhow had time to be convinced that Jesus was Messias, the Anointed.

42. Our Lord looks at him and tells him he is to be called Cephas (Peter: Rock). Our Lord does not explain this till long afterwards: but He is now beginning to act 'independently', not at the suggestion of others.

The Calling of Philip and Nathanael: 43-51

43. On the following day, he would go forth into Galilee: and he findeth Philip. And Jesus saith to him: Follow me.
44. Now Philip was of Bethsaida, the city of Andrew and Peter.
45. Philip findeth Nathanael and saith to him: We have found him of whom Moses, in the law and the prophets did write, Jesus the son of Joseph of Nazareth.
46. And Nathanael said to him: Can any thing of good come from Nazareth? Philip saith to him: Come and see.
47. Jesus saw Nathanael coming to him and he saith of him: Behold an Israelite indeed, in whom there is no guile.

---

43. 'Jesus decided to go—' We are not told when He started or arrived or at what moment He met Philip and Nathanael. Bethsaida was on the lake of Galilee (Mark 6: 45; Luke 9: 10). John gives the merest outline of events: He tells Philip abruptly to 'follow' Him, i.e. as disciple and not just to Galilee: Philip does so, and is able to tell Nathanael of a long conversation with Jesus and his conviction that followed from it. He does not say: 'the' son of Joseph, which would have implied Jesus was already known to them: but 'son of Joseph of Nazareth' suffices to indicate His Davidic descent. Nathanael is presumably the same as Bartholomew ('son of Tolmai') who is associated with Philip in the lists of Apostles (e.g. Matthew 10: 3).
46. Nathanael did not imply that Nazareth was a specially wicked place, but only that he, from Cana, held his neighbours in contempt, as often happens when men inhabit neighbouring townlets.
47. Our Lord says: '*There* is truly an Israelite!' i.e. one worthy of the name. The word may have some connection with the idea of simplicity, rectitude (cf. Gen. 25: 27). Crafty manoeuvering was almost a disease among orientals.

14

48. Nathanael saith to him: Whence knowest thou me? Jesus answered and said to him: Before that Philip called thee, when thou wast under the fig tree, I saw thee.

49. Nathanael answered him and said: Rabbi: Thou art the Son of God. Thou art the King of Israel.

50. Jesus answered and said to him: Because I said unto thee, I saw thee under the fig tree, thou believest: greater things than these shalt thou see.

51. And he saith to him: Amen, amen, I say to you, you shall see the heaven opened and the angels of God ascending and descending upon the Son of man.

---

48. Either: 'How do you know my name?' (but would not Philip have told Him whom he was bringing?): or, 'How can you have views about me?' Our Lord says that before ever Philip called him, while he was under 'the fig-tree', He had seen him. But we had heard nothing about a fig-tree; it seems clear that our Lord saw him there 'clairvoyantly': simply to have seen him at a distance would not have convinced him that He was Messias (the two expressions 'Son of God', 'King of Israel' will not have meant so far more than 'Messias'). Once more, John is not writing a full historical account of these early encounters between Jesus and the future Apostles, but describing the definite transition from the Baptist to Jesus: see 3: 22–30. Long afterwards there were those who had heard only of 'the baptism of John' (Acts 19: 3). St John is not despising the Baptist, but certainly is making it clear that he is no more the leading personage.

51. The repetition 'Amen, amen' is not in the Synoptists, but only in John, and on our Lord's own lips. We cannot point to any particular vision of angels 'ascending and descending' upon our Lord: we think that our Lord does not want Nathanael to base his faith on some simple portent like 'clairvoyance': he shall see greater things than that! He shall realize that all the host of heaven is at the service of Himself— the Son of Man. The 'picture' evokes the memory of Jacob's ladder (Gen. 28: 10–17): the expression 'Son of Man' is always on our Lord's own lips, save Acts 7: 5, when Stephen sees 'the Son of Man' standing at God's right hand. This title was not regarded as implying, definitely, the 'Messias', but it did emphasize our Lord's Humanity, and yet, somehow hint that He was above the rest of His fellow-men. See St Mark, Introd. p. xix. Cf. Dan. 7: 13 ff.

CHAPTER TWO

The Marriage at Cana: 1–11

1. And the third day, there was a marriage in Cana of Galilee: and the mother of Jesus was there.
2. And Jesus also was invited, and his disciples, to the marriage.
3. And the wine failing, the mother of Jesus saith to him: They have no wine.
4. And Jesus saith to her: Woman, what is that to me and to thee? My hour is not yet come.

The Prologue was, as we said, a great arch leading into the castle, with all the King's titles set forth in the escutcheon over the gate. The four episodes relating to the change from the Baptist, as central figure, to our Lord served as an outer court: and now John by means of two more episodes brings us to the great Court immediately preceding the castle of our Lord's doctrine itself.

1. 'The third day' probably means three days after the colloquy with Nathanael which, after all, may have taken place when our Lord had already gone much of the way to Galilee. Cana was Nathanael's home-town (21: 2) and it may be he who invited his new friends to the marriage, especially if he had learnt that our Lord's mother was a guest there. Cana was probably only a few miles from Nazareth, though the site is not certain. No doubt the arrival of several new guests accounted for the wine running short. Mary says briefly to her Son: 'They have no wine.'

4. In Aramaic as e.g. in Greek the word translated 'woman' was by no means curt or severe: anyone from a princess downward, for whom one had respect could be so addressed

5. His mother saith to the waiters: Whatsoever he shall say to you, do ye.

6. Now there were set there six water-pots of stone, according to the manner of the purifying of the Jews, containing two or three measures apiece.

7. Jesus saith to them: Fill the water-pots with water. And they filled them up to the brim.

8. And Jesus saith to them: Draw out now and carry to the chief steward of the feast. And they carried it.

9. And when the chief steward had tasted the water made wine and knew not whence it was, but the waiters knew who had drawn the water: the chief steward calleth the bridegroom,

10. And saith to him: Every man at first setteth forth good wine, and when men have well drunk, then that which is worse. But thou hast kept the good wine until now.

Τί ἐμοὶ καὶ σοί; literally: 'What to me and to thee?' 'What have I to do with thee?' (Authorized Version) is a misleading translation. In Matthew 8: 29; 2 Kings 16, 10 etc. the words show that we must here understand something like: 'Do not intervene! This is *My* affair!' and the expression receives its meaning from the tone of voice with which it is spoken. And what follows makes all clear—'My time (for working miracles) is not yet come.' Notice, first, that our Lady feels sure that He *will* do something to save the situation; and then, that He does in fact anticipate His 'hour' at her request. Our Lady, feeling sure it would be so, says to the servants: '*Whatever* He says to you, do it!' And indeed His order would seem strange. It is calculated that the six jars, holding two or three 'measures' each, would have accounted for between 100 and 150 gallons, assuming that all the contents were turned into wine and not only what was drawn out. What was not drunk, would presumably become the possession of the married couple.

8. The *architriklinos* was the man who supervised the service.

9, 10. This may have been a sort of respectful jest on his part: no

CHAPTER TWO

11. This beginning of miracles did Jesus in Cana of Galilee and manifested his glory. And his disciples believed in him.

The Cleansing of the Temple: 12–25

12. After this, he went down to Capharnaum, he and his mother and his brethren and his disciples: and they remained there not many days.
13. And the pasch of the Jews was at hand: and Jesus went up to Jerusalem.

---

custom is known according to which worse wine was served at the end of a feast.

11. 'Such was the beginning of the "signs" that Jesus did', showing thereby His 'glory', which must here mean His more than human power, so that His disciples believed yet more firmly in Him. We may be sure that John does not relate an event of history like this one without seeing in it a spiritual significance. He is approaching his central doctrine by showing our Lord as meaning to provide something as much better than the Jewish religion with all its ritual, as the good red wine was better than insipid water. In his next section, he indicates what the 'something' *is.*

12. It was only some time later that Jesus practically settled in Capharnaum (Matt. 4: 13; 9: 1; Mark 2: 1 and cf. John 6: 17 etc.); but by then Nazareth was hostile to him and so were His kinsfolk, and we never hear of Mary living in Capharnaum. This was but a visit of a few days. Why did He go there? We think it occurred on His return from Judea, perhaps because His new friends wanted Him to see their home-region.

13. A difficulty here consists in the Synoptists' (1) mentioning only one Pasch during our Lord's ministry, namely, that during which He died: and (2) placing a cleansing of the Temple during the preceding week. The first difficulty vanishes if we suppose that the Synoptists decided to describe our Lord's preaching only from the time of the Baptist's imprisonment and the silencing of the 'Voice'. The second would vanish if we suppose that there were two cleansings of

14. And he found in the temple them that sold oxen and sheep and doves, and the changers of money sitting.

15. And when he had made, as it were, a scourge of little cords, he drove them all out of the temple, the sheep also and the oxen: and the money of the changers he poured out, and the tables he overthrew.

16. And to them that sold doves he said: Take these things hence, and make not the house of my Father a house of traffic.

17. And his disciples remembered, that it was written: *The zeal of thy house hath eaten me up.*

---

the Temple: this cannot be disproved, but it seems to us unlikely that our Lord would have inaugurated His ministry by so drastic an action with nothing leading up to it. In Galilee, He entered almost imperceptibly upon His ministry, definitely unlike the sensational Baptist. The Evangelists did not write with strict regard for chronology. The Synoptists (especially St Matthew) group matters together (e.g. the parables) for convenience' sake, or because what they had reported made them think of some allied saying. There is, then, no objection to supposing, as in fact we do, that St John placed this episode here for spiritual reasons—i.e. to show *what* it was that our Lord provided so much better than the ancient Jewish system: instead of the Temple there would be *Himself.* The accounts in the Synoptists are in Matt. 21: 12–17; Mark 11: 15–19; Luke 19: 45–48.

14. In 'the Temple' means in the great outer court where requisites for sacrifice were sold. Two different words are used for 'money-changers' in verses 14 and 15 perhaps for variety's sake, or because there were two exchanges going on—small coins for larger ones, and Jewish coins (which alone were allowed in the Temple) for pagan coins brought by pilgrims. Only St John mentions the whip of 'small cords'—possibly they had been used to tie the lambs before sale, and our Lord picked them up: and only St Mark says that He would not allow the Temple-court to be used as a short cut by people carrying parcels. St John alone shows our Lord treating the

18. The Jews, therefore, answered, and said to him: What sign dost thou shew unto us, seeing thou dost these things?

19. Jesus answered and said to them: Destroy this temple; and in three days I will raise it up.

20. The Jews then said: Six and forty years was this temple in building; and wilt thou raise it up in three days?

21. But he spoke of the temple of his body.

22. When therefore he was risen again from the dead, his disciples remembered that he had said this: and they believed the scripture and the word that Jesus had said.

---

sellers of doves more gently: there was less chance of putting up the price of doves than of cattle: he does not actually quote, as the Synoptists do, Is. 56: 7; Jer. 7: 11; but his meaning is the same. The disciples however remember the enigmatic words of Ps. 68: 9: 'The zeal of Thy house hath eaten me up': we can easily say: 'I am devoured with zeal for' something: but the Psalm goes on: 'and upon me have fallen the insults of them that insult Thee': the Psalmist then must mean that his zeal for the Temple has but brought insult and disaster upon him. If the cleansing of the Temple took place during Holy Week, the conversation with the Jews would have its point, and our Lord's words might well have been quoted at His trial, though hardly if they had been spoken two or three years earlier.

18. The Temple officials, nervous lest a popular uprising should take place, ask what sign He gives to *them* to justify His behaviour.

19–22. His reply could not be properly understood at the time, though John may give his readers a hint by using the word 'raise it up' instead of the more natural 'rebuild it'. But as always, His hearers begin by taking Him in the most materialist sense: Herod the Great had begun to rebuild the Temple in the 18th year of his reign, presumably 20 or 19 B.C. '46 years' would bring us to A.D. 28. The whole rebuilding was not finished till A.D. 63. This prophecy, as many others,

23. Now when he was at Jerusalem, at the pasch, upon the festival day, many believed in his name, seeing his signs which he did.
24. But Jesus did not trust himself unto them: for that he knew all men.
25. And because he needed not that any should give testimony of man: for he knew what was in man.

---

was understood only when it was fulfilled, cf. 11: 12; 16: 17 ff. Of course our Lord was making no allusion to His own age.

23. 'In the feast' (so the Greek) means 'during the feast': the Pasch lasted a week. We are not told what 'signs' our Lord worked, nor precisely what kind of 'faith' in Him they produced.

24, 25. He would not 'trust Himself to them' must mean either that they would have been swept away by enthusiasm and tried to make Him declare Himself Messiah-King; or, much more probably, He would not yet 'trust' the whole truth about Himself to them: even the disciples were not for a long time able to assimilate it: He 'knew them all', and did not need anyone to explain their interior dispositions to Him: He knows what is 'in man', and understands us far better than we do ourselves.

CHAPTER THREE

Nicodemus (i): 1–15

1. And there was a man of the Pharisees, named Nicodemus, a ruler of the Jews.
2. This man came to Jesus by night and said to him: Rabbi, we know that thou art come a teacher from God; for no man can do these signs which thou dost, unless God be with him.
3. Jesus answered and said to him: Amen, amen, I say to thee, unless a man be born again, he cannot see the kingdom of God.
4. Nicodemus saith to him: How can a man be born when he is old? Can he enter a second time into his mother's womb and be born again?

---

1. Nicodemus (Greek names were not rare, especially among distinguished Jews) was not only a Pharisee but a member of the Sanhedrin, the Jewish 'government'.
2. He came at night, so as not to compromise himself. He begins courteously, naming Jesus 'Teacher', adding that 'we know', i.e. a group to which he belongs; or, it is known that: cf. 11; he admits that the 'signs' he has seen indicate a divine guarantee. Our Lord cuts short this prelude.
3. Unless a man be born 'anew', he cannot see the Kingdom of God. The Greek word ἄνωθεν is ambiguous: it can mean 'over again', or, 'from above', cf. 3: 31; 19: 11, 23.
4. Nicodemus chooses the obvious, 'materialist' sense: How can a man be born a second time, physically, when he is old? It was not necessary for him to say more than 'twice': but 'old' is more expressive if he were himself old.

5. Jesus answered: Amen, amen, I say to thee, unless a man be born again of water and the Holy Ghost, he cannot enter into the kingdom of God.

6. That which is born of the flesh is flesh: and that which is born of the Spirit is spirit.

7. Wonder not that I said to thee: You must be born again.

8. The Spirit breatheth where he will and thou hearest his voice: but thou knowest not whence he cometh and whither he goeth. So is every one that is born of the Spirit.

9. Nicodemus answered and said to him: How can these things be done?

10. Jesus answered and said to him: Art thou a master in Israel, and knowest not these things?

11. Amen, amen, I say to thee that we speak what we know and we testify what we have seen: and you receive not our testimony.

12. If I have spoken to you earthly things, and you believe not: how will you believe, if I shall speak to you heavenly things?

---

5. St John becomes explicit: one must be born 'of water and the Spirit' if one is to enter the Kingdom of God. The Council of Trent forbids us to take the 'water' as a mere metaphor: it refers to the Sacrament of Baptism (cf. Titus 3: 5), which is necessary (Mark 16: 16; Matt. 28: 19): but this New Birth of the New Man into a New World cannot but recall the account of the First Creation, when the Spirit of God brooded on the chaotic lifeless waters (Gen. 1: 2), especially as St John, in his Prologue, has *Genesis* clearly in his mind.

6. By 'flesh', St John is not contrasting body and soul; he means that our natural birth is no more than that: the Spirit is what alone can 'super-naturalize' us.

7, 8. Nicodemus does not grasp the idea of this spiritual birth: our Lord tells him not to be surprised: the wind is invisible (they may have been sitting on the house-top): you do not see its origin or end: by comparison, the Spirit (the word πνεῦμα is the same in each case) is invisible and its effect in the soul is invisible too.

9–12. Nicodemus desponds. 'How can that happen?' Our Lord,

13. And no man hath ascended into heaven, but he that descended from heaven, the Son of man who is in heaven.

14. And as Moses lifted up the serpent in the desert, so must the Son of man be lifted up:

15. That whosoever believeth in him may not perish, but may have life everlasting.

---

gently smiling at him, we may suppose, says: 'You are "the Master of Israel", and you don't know that?' (Nicodemus may have been a prominent authority, and nicknamed 'the Master'; possibly, 'of us two, *you* are obviously the Master!')

11. Why the abrupt use of the plural? The words are clearly given as our Lord's; yet He never speaks of Himself as 'we'. It may well be like the French *on*, or German *man*: 'I tell you—one says only what one knows, and witnesses only to what one has *seen*—yet you will not accept such witness!' 'Well', He resumes, 'If I have told you Jews things-of-earth, and you don't believe, how, should I tell you heavenly things, are you going to believe?' What are these 'earthly things'? We think, the simple yet lofty moral doctrine such as we read of in the Synoptists: if *that* is not accepted, how should a supernatural doctrine be listened to?

13–15. We think that these words are still to be regarded as spoken by our Lord, yet that St John's own thought is beginning to shine through them, until in verse 16 he begins to speak in his own person. The sentence is elliptical—'No one has climbed up to heaven (to see and be able to proclaim the "heavenly things" alluded to): He alone can proclaim things-of-heaven whose eternal existence is *in* heaven', 'and who has come down thence' to teach them to men. But our Lord adds what can but refer at least remotely to the saving death upon the cross: the brazen serpent was uplifted on a pole (Num. 21: 9), and the sick Israelites looked up towards it and God healed them: so should all have to look to Jesus, lifted high before their eyes, for their salvation.

Nicodemus (ii): 16–21

16. For God so loved the world, as to give his only begotten Son: that whosoever believeth in him may not perish, but may have life everlasting.

17. For God sent not his Son into the world, to judge the world: but that the world may be saved by him.

18. He that believeth in him is not judged. But he that doth not believe is already judged: because he believeth not in the name of the only begotten Son of God.

---

16. Our Lord's words have inspired John's reflections on them: God so loved the world—even this sinful world—that He gave His sole-begotten Son that all who believe in Him should not perish (the fate possible for all) but have (be forthwith in possession of) 'Eternal Life' (the key-word of John's gospel). What follows is difficult because the words for 'judgment', 'judge' (κρίσις : κρίνειν) are used in two senses. *Crisis* means a 'separation' (at the crisis of an illness the sick man recovers or fails to do so), but also, 'condemnation'.

17. God, who loved the world, did not send His Son into it to condemn it, but to save it. 'He who believes in Him is not being judged'—elsewhere, 'coming to Him' is equivalent to 'believing in Him': there is, then, no separation between the true believer and our Lord: similarly, 'he who does not believe is already in a state of separation because he is not believing . . .' (the two verbs are in the perfect and indicate a state, not an isolated act). It is by now certainly clear that St John is now making his own reflections, i.e. as to the state of the Jews after their rejection of our Lord: for they could neither be separated nor condemned if they had not yet been given their full chance of believing in and coming to Him. Remember that St John could not use inverted commas: we do not know how the (briefly summarized) talk with Nicodemus ended: it *shades off* into St John's own words.

19. And this is the judgment: Because the light is come into the world and men loved darkness rather than the light. For their works were evil.

20. For every one that doth evil hateth the light and cometh not to the light, that his works may not be reproved.

21. But he that doth truth cometh to the light, that his works may be made manifest: because they are done in God.

The Baptist's Abdication: 22–36

22. After these things, Jesus and his disciples came into the land of Judea: and there he abode with them and baptized.

19–21. We think that in verse 19 the 'Light' means the divine Light as such (see the Prologue); in 20, it is used as a general illustration—most people who do wrong try not to be found out. In 21, St John turns back towards the God-given light. Meanwhile, the *Crisis*, the 'division' (cf. Luke 2: 34) and *thereby* the judgment, at once takes place: men *prefer* the Dark to the Light. They do not believe: they do not come: they turn their backs and go away. We can now say that whoever acts according to the light that is in him, is 'coming to' the Lord: he could not do even that (*sicut oportet*: so as to be justified: Trent) without God's help. But when he fully believes, as St John says, he must proceed to the new Sacramental Birth of water and the Spirit. The gospel does not refer to infant baptism; but the practice of the Church and the development of the doctrine of baptism show that it can and should be administered.

22. Either this means that Jesus left Jerusalem for the country parts of Judea, or, as we think, John continues to present a series of significant scenes without regard to chronological sequence. In 4: 2 St John definitely says that Jesus himself did not baptize, but it was His disciples who did so: this 'baptism' did not differ from John's save in so far as it attracted men to follow Jesus as His 'disciples': it did not confer grace. John could therefore go on baptizing.

23. And John also was baptizing in Ennon near Salim: because there was much water there. And they came and were baptized.

24. For John was not yet cast into prison.

25. And there arose a question between some of John's disciples and the Jews, concerning purification.

26. And they came to John and said to him: Rabbi, he that was with thee beyond the Jordan, to whom thou gavest testimony: behold, he baptizeth and all men come to him.

27. John answered and said: A man cannot receive any thing, unless it be given him from heaven.

28. You yourselves do bear me witness that I said that I am not Christ, but that I am sent before him.

---

23. Ennon (Ainon) is evidently not near the Jordan, else his baptizing would not have had to be explained by saying that there were many waters there—i.e. springs or rivulets. There is no certainty where Ainon or Salim were.

25. Another reading is 'with *a* Jew': it is the more difficult alternative and so more likely to have been corrected; and it is odd to say that the Baptist's disciples were arguing with 'the Jews', since they too were Jews. The discussion is not said to be precisely about 'baptism', but 'purification', and it is suggested that there was some difference between baptism as administered by our Lord's disciples and that given by John and his. Possibly the Jews argued that the whole idea of exterior cleansing was useless and thought they had heard our Lord say so.

26. The Baptist's disciples, piqued, go to him and define our Lord, not as 'he whom you baptized' (St John does not relate the baptism), but as 'he to whom you bore witness' (1: 26–34). But if they recalled that the Baptist had placed Jesus so far above himself, what did they object to? Theirs was a loyal but petulant jealousy: 'everyone is going to him!'

27. 'A man cannot lay hold of, arrogate to himself, a task, position, vocation, other than what God has ordained for him.

29. He that hath the bride is the bridegroom: but the friend of the bridegroom, who standeth and heareth him, rejoiceth with joy because of the bridegroom's voice. This my joy therefore is fulfilled.

30. He must increase: but I must decrease.

31. He that cometh from above is above all. He that is of the earth, of the earth he is, and of the earth he speaketh. He that cometh from heaven is above all.

32. And what he hath seen and heard, that he testifieth: and no man receiveth his testimony.

33. He that hath received his testimony hath set to his seal that God is true.

34. For he whom God hath sent speaketh the words of God: for God doth not give the Spirit by measure.

---

28. You yourselves acknowledge that I said: "I am not the Christ, but was sent ahead of *Him*"' (i.e. of Jesus: the pronoun is ἐκείνου: had 'the Christ' been referred to, it should have been αὐτοῦ). But John is better than *resigned*. He loves our Lord, and not only does not resent taking a secondary place but has his special joy there. Only *one* can possess the bride—the bridegroom: but the 'bridegroom's friend', standing near, listens to the bridegroom and exults in *his* happiness. In the O.T., the People is often called the bride of the Lord: Jesus called Himself by the name 'Bridegroom' (Mark 2: 19; Matt. 9: 15; Luke 5: 34). To Him alone belong the souls of men: cf. too St Paul, and often in the Apocalypse. Hence despite verse 30, John's joy is full to overflowing (cf. 15: 11; 16: 24; 1 John 1: 4 etc.).

31. This verse and up to 36 are the Evangelist's thoughts inspired by what he has just related: cf. how the interview with Nicodemus passes into John's reflections (16–21); in fact the two passages could follow one another: John no doubt 'witnessed to' Jesus: but the Lord's words were incomparably superior as coming direct from 'above', i.e. heaven. Yet 'no one' (cf. 'all', 26) attends to Him (cf. 1: 10, 11).

33, 34. He who accepts Christ's witness attests, as though by sign

35. The Father loveth the Son: and he hath given all things into his hand.

36. He that believeth in the Son hath life everlasting: but he that believeth not the Son shall not see life: but the wrath of God abideth on him.

---

and seal, that God is truthful—*for* He whom God sent speaks the words of *God*—for He does not give the Spirit by measure: the *word* 'God' is probably added here to make an obscure sentence clearer. But it is still not evident who is the subject of 'give'. Perhaps it means that God pours His Spirit without stint upon His Messias who accordingly speaks the whole of God's revelation, not partially as the prophets did; or, that Christ Himself gives the Holy Ghost without stint to those who accept Him. So, Origen, quoting Joel 2: 28, and St Cyril of Alexandria.

35, 36. The same doctrine—the Father loves the Son and puts all things into His hands, and He on His side becomes the source of eternal life to all who believe in Him. The wrath of God 'remains' (D. 'abideth') on those who reject the Son (1 Cor. 15: 17; 1 Thess. 1: 10). All saving grace is given through the merits of Christ, even to those who are men of good will but have no explicit knowledge of Him.

CHAPTER FOUR

The Samaritan Woman (i): 1–6

1. When Jesus therefore understood that the Pharisees had heard that Jesus maketh more disciples and baptizeth *more* than John.
2. (Though Jesus *himself* did not baptize, but his disciples),
3. He left Judea and went again into Galilee.
4. And he was of necessity to pass through Samaria.
5. He cometh therefore to a city of Samaria, which is called Sichar, near the land which Jacob gave to his son Joseph.
6. Now Jacob's well was there. Jesus therefore, being wearied with his journey, sat thus on the well. It was about the sixth hour.

---

1. No suggestion that the Pharisees objected to our Lord's *doctrine*, but He was creating an even worse popular upheaval than John did.
4. The usual road from Judea to Galilee passed through Samaria, though a Jew would normally have avoided it. Samaritans were a mixed race of Hebrews and pagans; they kept only the earliest books of the O.T. and had a worship of their own in a temple on the neighbouring Mount Gerizim. Sichar was a small place near Sichem (today Nablus). Jacob gave land there to Joseph (Gen. 48: 22) and the well (still existing) was naturally called after Jacob.
6. 'He sat *thus*' (οὕτως) is almost a gesture—our Lord, exhausted, let Himself sink down, either sitting on the parapet or on the ground and leaning against it.

The 'source' or 'fountain' of Jacob flowed up deep down in the well and was far from filling it full (cf. 11). Palestinian women still let down pitchers by cords into wells leaving parallel grooves on the parapet.

The Samaritan Woman (ii): 7-15

7. There cometh a woman of Samaria, to draw water. Jesus saith to her: Give me to drink.

8. For his disciples were gone into the city to buy meats.

9. Then that Samaritan woman saith to him: How dost thou, being a Jew, ask of me to drink, who am a Samaritan woman? For the Jews do not communicate with the Samaritans.

10. Jesus answered and said to her: If thou didst know the gift of God and who he is that saith to thee: Give me to drink; thou perhaps wouldst have asked of him, and he would have given thee living water.

11. The woman saith to him: Sir, thou hast nothing wherein to draw, and the well is deep. From whence then hast thou living water?

12. Art thou greater than our father Jacob, who gave us the well and drank thereof, himself and his children and his cattle?

---

7. No doubt the disciples would have brought back a pitcher too, or a flask of wine.

9. She may have recognized Him as a Jew because of the Jewish fringe on His cloak or simply because of a difference in look, or pronunciation. The neighbourhood was specially disliked by Jews because so near to Gerizim and its rival temple and worship: and Sichem in particular was held to be dwelt in by a 'stupid folk' (λάος μωρός). This well is 32 metres deep: even when there had been much rain, the water was still (1924) about 10 metres below the top. Our Lord begins with a word of double meaning (as He did when talking to Nicodemus: (3: 3; cf. 6: 33))—'living water' can mean simply 'fresh water' (spring water as contrasted with water in a cistern), or, a water mysteriously alive. The woman naturally takes the more obvious meaning, as Nicodemus did. She is sarcastic —he has no pail—the well is deep—Jacob doubtless used pitchers—did *he* propose to manage without one?

10. Our Lord says: 'Had you but known the Gift of God, and who He is who is asking you to give Him to drink, it is *you*

13. Jesus answered and said to her: Whosoever drinketh of this water shall thirst again: but he that shall drink of the water that I will give him shall not thirst for ever.

14. But the water that I will give him shall become in him a fountain of water, springing up into life everlasting.

15. The woman saith to him: Sir, give me this water, that I may not thirst, nor come hither to draw.

The Samaritan Woman (iii): 16–26

16. Jesus saith to her: Go, call thy husband, and come hither.

17. The woman answered and said: I have no husband. Jesus said to her: Thou hast said well: I have no husband.

18. For thou hast had five husbands: and he whom thou now hast is not thy husband. This thou hast said truly.

19. The woman saith to him: Sir, I perceive that thou art a prophet.

20. Our fathers adored on this mountain: and you say that at Jerusalem is the place where men must adore.

---

who would have asked of Him and He would have given you "living water"!'.

13. He tries to lead her forward: anyone who drinks of this *sort* of water—from spring or from cistern—will thirst again; but the water that our Lord gives—super-natural Grace—is like a fountain in the soul; we shall not have laboriously to go and get some more: certainly we should always want to be in closer union with our Lord: but once Grace is 'in' our soul, that is 'Eternal Life' begun.

16. Our Lord, seeing that she cannot rise above the material meaning of His words, startles her (cf. Nathanael; 1: 48). We have only a 'skeleton outline', the 'key-sentences' of these discourses: but He has said enough to make her exclaim that He is a 'prophet', mysteriously 'clairvoyant'. She abruptly says that 'our ancestors' worshipped on this mountain (Gerizim), of which the lower slopes were visible from the well, 'but *you* say' that the place where people ought to

21. Jesus saith to her: Woman, believe me that the hour cometh, when you shall neither on this mountain, nor in Jerusalem, adore the Father.

22. You adore that which you know not: we adore that which we know. For salvation is of the Jews.

23. But the hour cometh and now is, when the true adorers shall adore the Father in spirit and in truth. For the Father also seeketh such to adore him.

24. God is a spirit: and they that adore him must adore him in spirit and in truth.

25. The woman saith to him: I know that the Messias cometh (who is called Christ): therefore, when he is come, he will tell us all things.

26. Jesus saith to her: I am he, who am speaking with thee.

---

worship is in Jerusalem. The priest Manasses (about 430 B.C.?) had built a rival temple on Gerizim; it had been destroyed in 129 B.C., but the Samaritans still maintained that Gerizim was the proper place for divine worship. Our Lord brushes aside the idea that the worship of God is in any sense 'localized'. He adds in parenthesis that no doubt a unique revelation was

22. given to the Hebrews and is preserved by their heirs, the Jews, and that from among the Jews salvation was to come; but all

23. the same the time had actually arrived when men should worship God 'spiritually' and 'truly'—i.e. in no misguided or limited way, as though they could give Him *full* worship in one place rather than another—and *that* is the sort of worship God is asking for, corresponding to His own 'spirituality' and, as we might say, 'omnipresence'.

25. The woman seems to shrug her shoulders: 'Ah, well, when Messias comes, he will explain everything!' Our Lord's

26. declaration that *He is* the Messias seems to clash with His frequent prohibition in the Synoptists of any public claim to Messiah-hood: but St John makes our Lord's discourses with individuals, or smaller groups, lead up to this (Nicodemus; the man who had been born blind, 9: 37; Martha, 11: 25: and see below, 8: 31 to the end of the chapter).

The Samaritan Woman (iv): 27–42

27. And immediately his disciples came. And they wondered that he talked with the woman. Yet no man said: What seekest thou? Or: Why talkest thou with her?

28. The woman therefore left her waterpot and went her way into the city and saith to the men there:

29. Come, and see a man who has told me all things whatsoever I have done. Is not he the Christ?

30. They went therefore out of the city and came unto him.

31. In the mean time the disciples prayed him, saying: Rabbi, eat.

32. But he said to them: I have meat to eat which you know not.

33. The disciples therefore said one to another: Hath any man brought him to eat?

34. Jesus saith to them: My meat is to do the will of him that sent me, that I may perfect his work.

---

27. 'Immediately': i.e. 'at this point'. Read: 'a woman', not 'the'. It is still considered out of place, in the East, for a man to enter into casual conversation with a woman: the disciples' feeling of respect prevent their asking Him what He was

28, 29. talking to her about. As for her, she was more excited than she had seemed: she left the pitcher behind, and ran off to ask if this might not be the Messias? 'All that ever I did'—a wild exaggeration; or, St John may have just indicated the topic of a much longer talk.

30. They 'went out of the town' (aorist), and 'took their way to' Jesus (imperfect).

31. 'The meantime', i.e. between the departure of the woman and the arrival of the Samaritans.

32. It is not rare that a strong spiritual experience takes away all wish for food or drink.

34. The work of God has been begun, but our Lord foresees the multitudes that only await the Apostolate in order to be converted. He quotes a current 'proverb' (see 37)—'Four

35. Do not you say: There are yet four months, and then the harvest cometh? Behold, I say to you, lift up your eyes, and see the countries. For they are white already to harvest.

36. And he that reapeth receiveth wages and gathereth fruit unto life everlasting: that both he that soweth and he that reapeth may rejoice together.

37. For in this is the saying true: That it is one man that soweth, and it is another that reapeth.

38. I have sent you to reap that in which you did not labour. Others have laboured: and you have entered into their labours.

---

months yet, and then the harvest comes!' but says forthwith: 'Look! The fields are *already* white for harvesting!' (In England, we might say 'gold'; but apparently in the dry land of Palestine 'white' would be a more natural word.)

33–37. Our Lord, again looking into the future, sees the reapers receiving a wage and gathering grain 'unto eternal life', so that He, the Sower, rejoices along with them—'Yes', He adds, 'for in *this* the proverb is verified: "One man reaps what another man has sown." I have sent you to reap what has cost you no toil. Others . . . have toiled, and you have entered into (profited by) their toil.' It is our Lord's wonderful modesty and consideration which make Him say 'others' instead of 'I'. True, the reapers shall have 'a reward' for the work they shall have done, but none of it *could* have been done without the merits of the divine Sower, Christ. Our Lord quotes a proverb (which, we hold, had nothing to do with the season of the year which it then was) and no doubt He spoke it in Aramaic. But St John, writing for Greek readers, puts at least the first half into so perfect an iambic verse—containing even a rhyme between the middle and last syllables—that it is hard to think he did so unintentionally: ἔτι τετράμηνος, καὶ θερισμὸς ἔρχεται: we can translate into a somewhat similar rhythm: 'Foúr months yét, and thén the hárvest cómes!' The second half would correspond, in English, thus—'And one man reáps where another mán has

36

39. Now of that city many of the Samaritans believed in him, for the word of the woman giving testimony: He told me all things whatsoever I have done.

40. So when the Samaritans were come to him, they desired that he would tarry there. And he abode there two days.

41. And many more believed in him, because of his own word.

42. And they said to the woman: We now believe, not for the saying: for we ourselves have heard him and know that this is indeed the Saviour of the world.

Return to Galilee: 43–45

43. Now after two days, he departed thence and went into Galilee.

44. For Jesus himself gave testimony that a prophet hath no honour in his own country.

---

sówn;' but in Greek, this second half would need rearrangement to become fully rhythmic.

39. 'Believed.' Probably, at first, not more than that He was a mysterious person—a 'prophet'—possibly the Messias. But having actually met Him, they believed no more on hearsay ('thy talk' need not be contemptuous—'thy chatter'), but from His own lips. 'The Saviour of the world' is however a startling expression in Samaritan speech unless there were numerous Gentiles mixed up with the Samaritan citizens: even so, it is not possible to be sure what '*Saviour* of the *world*' will have meant, or would have meant on the lips even of Jews.

43, 44. It is impossible to see an exact logical connection between these sentences. I have no doubt that 'his own fatherland' means Galilee and not Judea though our Lord was born in Bethlehem. His parents' home was Nazareth, and there He lived, or (in a sense) at Capharnaum which came to be called 'His' town (Matt. 9: 1), but Mark 6: 1 definitely contrasts it with 'His own country', i.e. Nazareth. So one would expect

44. 'though', not 'for'. And then John says that the Galileans *did* 'receive', i.e. welcome Him. Perhaps we may fill out a

45. And when he was come into Galilee, the Galileans received him, having seen all the things he had done at Jerusalem on the festival day: for they also went to the festival day.

The Cure of the Ruler's Son: 46–54

46. He came again therefore into Cana of Galilee, where he made the water wine. And there was a certain ruler, whose son was sick at Capharnaum.

47. He having heard that Jesus was come from Judea into Galilee, went to him and prayed him to come down and heal his son: for he was at the point of death.

48. Jesus therefore said to him: Unless you see signs and wonders, you believe not.

49. The ruler saith to him: Lord, come down before that my son die.

50. Jesus saith to him: Go thy way. Thy son liveth. The man believed the word which Jesus said to him and went his way.

---

rapidly written paragraph thus—'He went into Galilee (which was surprising) for He Himself ($a\vec{v}\tau\acute{o}s$) had witnessed that a prophet had no honour in his own country (Mark 6: 4; Matt. 13: 57; Luke 4: 24). But (some of) the Galileans had seen what He did in Jerusalem and *therefore* welcomed Him.' We can say that the passage was hastily written, as being a mere link between two important and significant episodes— the story of the Samaritaness and the following miracle worked (probably) on behalf of a pagan.

46. The Vulgate *regulus* translates the Greek $\beta a \sigma \iota \lambda \iota \kappa \acute{o}s$ which is not so good as $\beta a \sigma \iota \lambda \iota \sigma \kappa \acute{o}s$, a 'court official' (in the service of Herod Antipas who, though only a tetrarch, could be flattered by the name 'King').

48. Our Lord uses the plural: 'You people . . .': this does not imply that the official was a Jew. 'Marvel' ($\tau\acute{e}\rho a s$), only here, in John. The official insists, not without pathos—'lest my little boy die!' And his faith earns for him our Lord's quick answer: 'Off with you! Your son is alive!'

51. And as he was going down, his servants met him: and they brought word, saying, that his son lived.

52. He asked therefore of them the hour wherein he grew better. And they said to him: Yesterday, at the seventh hour, the fever left him.

53. The father therefore knew that it was at the same hour that Jesus said to him: Thy son liveth. And himself believed, and his whole house.

54. This *is* again the second miracle that Jesus did, when he was come out of Judea into Galilee.

---

51. It is not certain where Cana was, or even if it was exactly there that our Lord was lodging. In any case, there was an abrupt descent to Capharnaum, hence the words: 'Come down!' and 'as he was going down'.

52. The seventh hour was about our one o'clock P.M. We might have expected the father to have started at once for home; he would have had plenty of time to ride the 20 miles or so between Cana and Capharnaum. Yet *if* he accepted with full faith the words of our Lord, it would have been in keeping with oriental hospitality that he should have been asked to spend the night at Cana, and have agreed to do so, and not have started home before daybreak.—At first sight one might think that this was a different version of the miracle related in Matt. 8: 5–13 and Luke 7: 1–10: in each case the sick person is at Capharnaum; the petition is addressed to our Lord at a distance and the cure effected without His presence: the 'court official' might have the post of 'centurion'; but the differences are considerable, and the faith of the pagan centurion is more emphasized in Matt. and Luke than in John, and also his deep humility. We do not think certainty is obtainable: anyhow, the lesson is identical: our Lord does not need to be physically present to exercise His power: but He will do so, if asked with urgent humble faith.

CHAPTER FIVE

The Cure of a Paralytic (i): 1–9

1. After these things was a festival day of the Jews: and Jesus went up to Jerusalem.
2. Now there is at Jerusalem a pond, *called* Probatica, which in Hebrew is named Bethsaida, having five porches.
3. In these lay a great multitude of sick, of blind, of lame, of withered: waiting for the moving of the water.

---

1. 'A festival day' would be a strange way of describing the Pasch: no other feast seems suitable save that of Pentecost: but certainty cannot be reached.
2. The best reading is 'by the Sheep-Gate'; ἐπὶ τῇ προβατικῇ: the pool was not called 'Probatica' but probably Bezatha, 'ditch', 'cutting' (as we speak of railway-cuttings): at the N.E. of the old City there was in fact a new quarter of the town separated from the older by such a 'ditch', which had derived its name—'Newditch'—from it. In London, after all, Shoreditch exists. St John, saying that the 'pool' *is* there, need not have been 'visualizing' a building destroyed some 20 years ago, for though the Romans broke down the city wall and Gate, they may have preserved (or even, as has been suggested, rebuilt) an edifice surrounding a source of such utility. Origen says that the 'pool' acquired the name 'Sheep' because sheep were brought there before festival-sacrifices and their entrails, after slaughter, washed in it, and (most important) that it had porticos on each of its four sides and another across the middle; and excavations have indeed found
3. the pool with its five-fold colonnade. In verse 3, 'waiting for the motion of the waters' is omitted in several but not most

4. And an angel of the Lord descended at certain times into the pond and the water was moved. And he that went down first into the pond after the motion of the water was made whole of whatsoever infirmity he lay under.

5. And there was a certain man there that had been eight and thirty years under his infirmity.

6. Him when Jesus had seen lying, and knew that he had been now a long time, he saith to him: Wilt thou be made whole?

7. The infirm man answered him: Sir, I have no man, when the water is troubled, to put me into the pond. For whilst I am coming, another goeth down before me.

---

4. MSS., and may well be genuine though verse 4 almost certainly is not. Not a few examples of intermittent radio-active sources could be quoted: pagans thought that the *genius loci* caused the waters to bubble up—even violently, as we see springs in New Zealand doing; a Jew would have assumed the action of an angel: it seems that the uprush of water at the Probatica lasted but for a moment, since it became thought that only one sick person was cured; also the legend had led to all sorts of sick people expecting a cure.

5. '38 years' might suggest to a Jew of that time that the illness was still curable: '40 years' would mark a final point beyond which nothing could be hoped.

6. St John as usual provides only the merest outline of the story. Why was our Lord there? why did He single out this man for notice? His words: 'Do you want to get well?' must have implied the question: 'How is it that by now you are not cured?' For the man's answer, that he can get no one to help him in first, explains why he, being friendless, had no chance in a kind of general scramble. Perhaps the water gushed up only in one place. But our Lord extricates the poor man who was hoping still against hope, from the superstition that had come to surround a natural curative phenomenon. Our Lord authoritatively bids him pick up his mattress and walk.

8. Jesus saith to him: Arise, take up thy bed and walk.

9. And immediately the man was made whole: and he took up his bed and walked. And it was the sabbath that day..

The Cure of a Paralytic (ii): 10–15

10. The Jews therefore said to him that was healed: It is the sabbath. It is not lawful for thee to take up thy bed.

11. He answered them: He that made me whole, he said to me: Take up thy bed and walk.

12. They asked him therefore: Who is that man who said to thee: Take up thy bed and walk?

13. But he who was healed knew not who it was; for Jesus went aside from the multitude standing in the place.

14. Afterwards, Jesus findeth him in the temple and saith to him: Behold thou art made whole: sin no more, lest some worse thing happen to thee.

15. The man went his way and told the Jews that it was Jesus who had made him whole.

---

8. And at once the man was cured, picked up the mat (aorist) and began to walk about (imperfect), though it was a sabbath.

10. In Jer. 17: 21 ff. this prohibition can be found, but it seems to allude to carrying burdens into or out of the city. Our Lord was ready to disregard such detailed vetos, but was not likely to order another to do what would get him into grave trouble. 'The Jews', then, were Pharisees of the more rigid sort.

14. This suggests that some long-ago sin had started the man's sickness: the 'worse thing' need not mean a relapse into graver illness, but that to sin after so great a favour might indeed imperil his soul.

15. The man does not mean to make trouble for Jesus, but presumably thinks the 'Jews' will join with him in gratitude.

The Works of Jesus are the Works of His Father: 16–23

16. Therefore did the Jews persecute Jesus, because he did these things on the sabbath.

17. But Jesus answered them: My Father worketh until now; and I work.

18. Hereupon therefore the Jews sought the more to kill him, because he did not only break the sabbath but also said God was his Father, making himself equal to God.

19. Then Jesus answered and said to them: Amen, amen, I say unto you, the Son cannot do any thing of himself, but what he seeth the Father doing: for what things soever he doth, these the Son also doth in like manner.

---

16. Read: 'And this is why the Jews persecuted Jesus—because He used to do these (i.e. such) acts on the sabbath.' This refers not merely to the incident just related, but to what Jesus not seldom did on the sabbath.

17. The point is, not that the Sabbath is abolished, but that Jesus, by good actions, is not violating the Sabbath any more than God is. For the 'Sabbath-rest' of *Genesis* marked the end of the process of creation. God continues to work beneficently and providentially ever since, and so, therefore, Jesus may do and does. (He could even have quoted the up-gushing of the curative spring, since the Jews no doubt saw in that a divine action!)

18. Our translation omits ἴδιον: 'makes God *His own* Father', His Father in a unique way which was to make Himself equal to God—a blasphemy; so 'all the more' did they resolve that He must die.

19. What follows is not a detached 'sermon' in no way connected with the situation and what had just been said: but (a) the Evangelist had not been present like a stenographer recording our Lord word for word, and anyhow (b) our Lord did not say everything all at once. He does not say forthwith: 'I am God': but, the Son does not act 'independently': as He sees

20. For the Father loveth the Son and sheweth him all things which himself doth: and greater works than these will he shew him, that you may wonder.

21. For as the Father raiseth up the dead and giveth life: so the Son also giveth life to whom he will.

22. For neither doth the Father judge any man: but hath given all judgment to the Son.

23. That all men may honour the Son, as they honour the Father. He who honoureth not the Son honoureth not the Father who hath sent him.

Our Lord foretells a Resurrection of Judgment: 24–29

24. Amen, amen, I say unto you that he who heareth my word and believeth him that sent me hath life everlasting and cometh not into judgment, but is passed from death to life.

His Father acting, so He, too, acts. But *why* does He thus 'know' the Father? Because the Father loves Him (cf. 3: 35)

20. and shows Him all that He does, and so, far greater things than these (bodily miracles) shall be revealed, and 'then indeed you may wonder!' (cf. 1: 50). What will these 'greater things' be? The bringing to life that which was 'dead' (or non-existent): God can bring the dead to life (Is. 26: 19; Dan. 12: 2 etc.): and the Son can give that 'Eternal Life'—the theme of the whole gospel—without which a soul is supernaturally dead.

22. We meet again the word *Crisis*, judgment, which we saw means either 'judgment' or 'separation' or hovers between the two. In 3: 17 our Lord says that He was not sent to 'judge', condemn, but to save: yet here we find that 'judgment' is entirely handed over to the Son, that is, here, to the Incarnate Son: according as a man does honour to Him, he does honour to God and is saved. For—

24. to hear, to 'come to', to believe in, mean the same thing in this gospel—an adherence of mind and will to Jesus, the Son of God. He who thus believes is forthwith in possession of

44

25. Amen, amen, I say unto you, that the hour cometh, and now is, when the dead shall hear the voice of the Son of God: and they that hear shall live.

26. For as the Father hath life in himself, so he hath given to the Son also to have life in himself.

27. And he hath given him power to do judgment, because he is the Son of man.

28. Wonder not at this: for the hour cometh, wherein all that are in the graves shall hear the voice of the Son of God.

29. And they that have done good things shall come forth unto the ressurrection of life, but they that have done evil unto the resurrection of judgment.

The Witness of the Baptist and of the Scriptures: 30–47

30. I cannot of myself do any thing. As I hear, so I judge. And my judgment is just: because I seek not my own will, but the will of him that sent me.

'eternal life'; he is not going towards 'judgment'—separation and a consequent condemnation, but he has crossed from death into Life.

25. Our Lord insists that the time has actually arrived when the 'dead' shall hear the voice of the Son of God and those who shall have listened to it shall live.

26, 27. The Father is the very source of life, and *grants* to the Son—inasmuch as He is Son of Man (i.e. human)—to have in Himself and to dispense Life, and to judge mankind.

28, 29. Our Lord tells His hearers not to be astonished (as they obviously were) by what He has said: the time will come (He does not here add 'and now *is*'), when *all*, even the physically dead, shall rise—the righteous, to a resurrection that means Life; evil-doers—He cannot exactly say 'to a resurrection of death', but, 'to a resurrection of judgment'—condemnation and separation for ever.

30. This verse both refers to what has been said and leads up to what follows. Jesus does not act independently of the Father:

31. If I bear witness of myself, my witness is not true.

32. There is another that beareth witness of me: and I know that the witness which he witnesseth of me is true.

33. You sent to John: and he gave testimony to the truth.

34. But I receive not testimony from man: but I say these things, that you may be saved.

35. He was a burning and a shining light: and you were willing for a time to rejoice in his light.

36. But I have a greater testimony than that of John: for the works which the Father hath given me to perfect, the works themselves which I do, give testimony of me, that the Father hath sent me.

37. And the Father himself who hath sent me hath given testimony of me: neither have you heard his voice at any time, nor seen his shape.

38. And you have not his word abiding in you: for whom he hath sent, him you believe not.

---

but His verdicts are righteous *because* He does not seek His own will but that of Him by whom He is sent. What are His 'credentials'?

31. If He were merely asserting His own credibility, no one could rely on Him.

32. He declares, as it were in parenthesis, that Another bears witness to Him—that is, God: but though *He* is sure that God is always supporting Him, this inner consciousness would not satisfy *them*. To what witness, then, shall He appeal?

33–35. The Baptist's? The Jews had sent to him and should have believed him.

34. A parenthesis: '*You* sent to him; but *I* do not rest My claim on any human witness: I refer to John for *your* sakes.'

35–36a. John was indeed the burning shining lamp—*you* were content for a while with his prophecies about the coming Messias: but *I* have a greater witness than his—the works that I do!

36b–38. 'My Father granted them to Me that I should carry them out—bring them to a point such as to render them a valid proof.' What follows is obscure: I think it means that God

39. Search the scriptures: for you think in them to have life everlasting. And the same are they that give testimony of me.

40. And you will not come to me that you may have life.

41. I receive not glory from men.

42. But I know you, that you have not the love of God in you.

43. I am come in the name of my Father, and you receive me not: if another shall come in his own name, him you will receive.

44. How can you believe, who receive glory one from another: and the glory which is from God alone, you do not seek?

---

has continuously been witnessing to His Son—true, you have never heard His voice nor seen His face (*that*, you could not expect: God is a pure Spirit, inaudible to ears and invisible to eyes), *but*, you have not His word, i.e. the way in which He does speak to souls, *abiding* in you; your interior ears are not open to His communications; else, you would have believed in Him whom He sent, which you do not!

39, 40. Probably: 'You search, study, the Scriptures (indicative; not imperative), because you think that *in them*, in the Law, you have eternal life: yet it is *they*—those very Scriptures, that are the witnesses to *Me*—yet you will not come to *Me* to have eternal life!'

41–47. These verses explain *why* the Jews do not come to Him. First, Jesus is not seeking recognition from them out of vanity —no! He seeks no glory from men! And *they* have no true love for God in them; they love the world and want a worldly Messias; therefore they cannot see God's emissary in Him. *He* comes in the name of God (and does 'works of God'); yet they will not accept Him. Others come in their own name (cf. Matt. 24: 24; Mark 13: 22) and them the Jews accept, though even (our Lord implies) if they claim to come from God, their claim fails to justify itself.

44. In fact, how *could* they believe, since what they seek is mutual approbation—not that which comes from God alone (probably, read 'from the One', God, who is unique).

45. Think not that I will accuse you to the Father. There is one that accuseth you, Moses, in whom you trust.

46. For if you did believe Moses, you would perhaps believe me also: for he wrote of me.

47. But if you do not believe his writings, how will you believe my words?

45–47. Our Lord, their Judge, is not going to be their 'prosecutor'. Moses suffices as their accuser. Moses had written about the future Salvation (e.g. Gen. 3: 15; 12: 3; 49: 10) and had as it were guaranteed the Prophets beforehand. Our Lord implies that they had shut their eyes to all save the Law as laid down by Moses and expounded by later teachers. But only minds specially guided by the Holy Spirit would have recognized, in Jesus, anything that Moses had explicitly or implicitly foretold. We may ask how the Jews can have followed a speech, at first hearing, of which we find it hard to follow the thread, or to decide on the exact meaning of certain phrases, even after re-reading it many times. First, our Lord must have been often interrupted. No oriental group, especially when strong feelings have been aroused, will listen for long in silence: hence the thread may often have been broken. Then, without falsifying what our Lord said, St John may have omitted links between sentences, or included what was said at other times— compare the treatment of the Beatitudes and the 'Eschatological Discourse' by St Matthew and St Luke. The essence of the doctrine here expressed is in Matt. 11: 25–27, and Luke 10: 21–22: in Mark, Jesus is throughout 'Son of God' in a unique way. Here, we are taught the identity of His life with the Father's (21), His works are God's works (19): He should be honoured as God is (23). Yet all this is true of Christ, true Man, and sent by God.

NOTE

Many hold that Chapter 5 should follow Chapter 6. How could such a transposition take place? Ancient books were made either by sticking one piece of papyrus on to the end of another, so as to make a roll: or else one page of writing was stitched to another so as to form a book, much as ours are: such a book is called a *codex*. All our pre-3rd-century papyri now surviving are in codex form; but so far they number only 8. But in the 3rd century we have 6 Christian rolls against 34 codices; in the 4th, 6 rolls against 62 codices. So the probability is that the Gospels were first written in codex form, though not on pages already stitched together, but on loose sheets. Now if a number of sheets had been stitched together so as to form a packet, it is easy to see how such packets could be put into a wrong order if e.g. they were knocked off a table and picked up again. So too a single sheet might be blown off and picked up and misplaced. But, pages were usually *numbered*: how, then, could they have been misplaced? We do not know that they were always numbered: and it is far from unknown that even a numbered sheet may find its way into a wrong place (this in fact happened twice to the typed pages of the present book). Smaller misplacements may have been due to a copyist having missed out a line or two and inserted them later, or in other ways to which students of ancient MSS. are accustomed. Possible instances of this are suggested in the Notes. Some reasons for supposing that Chapter 5 ought to follow Chapter 6 are, that Jesus at the end of Chapter 4 is in Galilee and that Chapter 6 begins by assuming that He is there: in 7: 23, He alludes to the cure of the paralytic on a sabbath as if it was fresh in men's memories, as it would be if Chapter 5 had closely preceded 7: Matt. and Mark suggest that the multiplication of bread occurred at once after the death of the Baptist, but in John 5: 35 he seems to have died a considerable time before. We are not fully convinced by these and other arguments of which the second seems to us the weightiest: but since St John was not writing strictly a biography attending to accurate chronology, the cure of the paralytic may have been fresh in *his* mind even if it had happened several months ago, for to him it had happened only a few *pages* ago.

CHAPTER SIX

The Multiplication of Bread: 1–15

1. After these things, Jesus went over the sea of Galilee, which is that of Tiberias.
2. And a great multitude followed him, because they saw the miracles which he did on them that were diseased.
3. Jesus therefore went up into a mountain: and there he sat with his disciples.
4. Now the pasch, the festival day of the Jews, was near at hand.

---

1. Cf. Matt. 14: 13–21: Mark 6: 31–44; Luke 9: 10b–17. If this chapter is in its proper place, we have to *assume* a return from Jerusalem to Galilee: but if Chapter 6 follows Chapter 4 Jesus is already in Galilee and it was quite natural to say, without explanation, that He crossed the Lake.
2. A crowd was now habitually following Him (imperfect) because of the miracles which St John by now assumes were frequent.
3. Jesus climbs some distance up 'the mountain'—all the east coast of the Lake was mountainous—and 'sat down', probably, we think, to rest (cf. Mark 6: 31 rather than Matt. 15: 29).
4. Why does St John mention the imminent Pasch? If he wants to 'date' an event, he does so at the beginning of his account of it (cf. 5: 1; 7: 2 etc.). Since he sees in the multiplication of bread the 'starting-point' for the great Eucharistic doctrine of this chapter, and since the Eucharist did indeed replace the Pasch, we may think that his mention of Paschal-tide occurring just then was due to his seeing in it a happy and significant coincidence.

5. When Jesus therefore had lifted up his eyes and seen that a very great multitude cometh to him, he said to Philip: Whence shall we buy bread, that these may eat?

6. And this he said to try him: for he himself knew what he would do.

7. Philip answered him: Two hundred pennyworth of bread is not sufficient for them, that every one may take a little.

8. One of his disciples, Andrew, the brother of Simon Peter, saith to him:

9. There is a boy here that hath five barley loaves and two fishes. But what are these among so many?

10. Then Jesus said: Make the men sit down. Now, there was much grass in the place. The men therefore sat down, in number about five thousand.

11. And Jesus took the loaves: and when he had given thanks, he distributed to them that were set down. In like manner also of the fishes, as much as they would.

12. And when they were filled, he said to his disciples: Gather up the fragments that remain, lest they be lost.

13. They gathered up therefore and filled twelve baskets with the fragments of the five barley loaves which remained over and above to them that had eaten.

---

5. St John goes straight to the feeding of the crowds: he has shown Jesus *noticing* the crowds below, as being true Man; in verse 6 he is careful not to let us think that this limited His divine knowledge.

7. 200 denarii would be a man's wage for 200 days of work.

8. Only St John mentions Philip and Andrew by name, or says that the loaves were of barley-meal—the food of the poorest class.

10. This suggests that there was not much grass elsewhere.

11. St John does not mention our Lord's looking upwards, nor breaking the bread; the miracle looks forward to the Eucharist, but is not modelled upon it.

12, 13. It was a Jewish custom to collect any fragments of food that might have fallen to the ground: apparently each of the

14. Now those men, when they had seen what a miracle Jesus had done, said: This is of a truth the prophet that is to come into the world.

15. Jesus therefore, when he knew that they would come to take him by force and make him king, fled again into the mountain, himself alone.

Jesus walks upon the water: 16–24

16. And when evening was come, his disciples went down to the sea.

17. And when they had gone up into a ship, they went over the sea to Capharnaum. And it was now dark: and Jesus was not come unto them.

18. And the sea arose, by reason of a great wind that blew.

Twelve found a big basket (κόφινος) which he filled with the bread and fish left over.

14, 15. The previous miracles had set the crowds in motion: *this* sign proves to them that Jesus is indeed the Prophet whom apparently the people, though not the Pharisees (cf. 1: 24), identified with the Messias, and whom they proposed to proclaim King. The word 'again' (πάλιν) need create no difficulty. Our Lord may well have come part of the way down the mountain-side and now climbs back again: possibly St John remembers that Jesus had already sought a mountain for retreat and rest or because of the execution of the Baptist (Mark 6: 31; Matt. 14: 13; Luke 9: 10).

16. We think that the order of events was as follows—our Lord climbed some way up the mountain and then part of the way down to the place reached by the crowds and worked His miracle. Then, as it drew towards evening (Luke 9: 12), that is, 3 P.M. onwards, our Lord began to send the people away (Mark 6: 45; Matt. 14: 22); but the more enthusiastic among them wished to carry Him off as king, so He fled back to the higher parts of the hills. He must have told the disciples to start without Him, for they did in fact begin to row towards Capharnaum, night having now fully fallen, and Jesus still being absent.

19. When they had rowed therefore about five and twenty or thirty furlongs, they see Jesus walking upon the sea and drawing nigh to the ship. And they were afraid.

20. But he saith to them: It is I. Be not afraid.

21. They were willing therefore to take him into the ship. And presently the ship was at the land to which they were going.

22. The next day, the multitude that stood on the other side of the sea saw that there was no other ship there but one: and that Jesus had not entered into the ship with his disciples, but that his disciples were gone away alone.

23. But other ships came in from Tiberias, nigh unto the place where they had eaten the bread, the Lord giving thanks.

24. When therefore the multitude saw that Jesus was not there, nor his disciples, they took shipping and came to Capharnaum, seeking for Jesus.

The Eucharistic Discourse (i): 25–34

25. And when they had found him on the other side of the sea, they said to him: Rabbi, when camest thou hither?

19–21. St John does not say they took our Lord for a ghost, but suggests that He was the cause of their fear, and only after hesitation they 'decided' to 'take Him into the ship', which 'forthwith' ($\epsilon\vartheta\theta\epsilon\omega\varsigma$) found itself at the shore for which they were making: St Matthew and St Mark note that the storm was calmed; they may, in the dark, have all but reached the land; or, St John may suggest that this quick arrival was a further miracle.

22–24. The construction is not easy. The meaning must be that the crowds (who had come on foot) realized that there *had been* only one boat, that the disciples had gone away in it, and that Jesus was not with them. Presumably some went one way, others in another, looking for Jesus, but other boats (probably fishing-boats) arrived from Tiberias, and those who were still near the shore persuaded these boats to take them back, not to Tiberias, but to Capharnaum where our Lord so often stayed.

25. 'When?' They might have said: 'How?' They had come as

26. Jesus answered them and said: Amen, amen, I say to you, you seek me, not because you have seen miracles, but because you did eat of the loaves and were filled.

27. Labour not for the meat which perisheth, but for that which endureth unto life everlasting, which the Son of man will give you. For him hath God, the Father, sealed.

28. They said therefore unto him: What shall we do, that we may work the works of God?

29. Jesus answered and said to them: This is the work of God, that you believe in him whom he hath sent.

30. They said therefore to him: What sign therefore dost thou shew that we may see and may believe thee? What dost thou work?

---

soon as they could: Jesus had *not* left in the only boat across the water: when, therefore, and how, had He come? No answer to this is given, because as usual John moves quickly to the significant points of a discourse.

26. Our Lord rebukes them—not that they had failed to see a *miracle*, since it had sufficed to make them try to capture Him for king, but because they had had their fill of miraculous bread and did not see that this was a *sign*: to decide to make Him king was as materialistic as to be hungry for mere bread.

27. A crucial verse. 'Work, not for food that perishes by the mere eating, but for the food which lasts—into Eternal Life!' The key-note of the Gospel has again been struck (cf. 4: 14): and this Life the Son of Man is offering you (better than 'shall offer', as though the Eucharist were already being spoken of) —the Father 'sealed' Him, went guarantee for Him, doubtless in many ways, but here the power of miracle-working is meant (5: 36).

28. The Law had told them what God wished them to do: evidently Jesus is demanding something more—what then is it?

29. The one divine 'work' that He does demand is that they should 'believe in Him—Him whom "*He*" (ἐκεῖνος) sent.

30. Astonishing question, if the men had seen the multiplication

54

31. Our fathers did eat manna in the desert, as it is written: *He gave them bread from heaven to eat.*

32. Then Jesus said to them: Amen, amen, I say to you; Moses gave you not bread from heaven, but my Father giveth you the true bread from heaven.

33. For the bread of God is that which cometh down from heaven and giveth life to the world.

34. They said therefore unto him: Lord, give us always this bread.

The Eucharistic Discourse (ii): 35–52

35. And Jesus said to them: I am the bread of life. He that cometh to me shall not hunger: and he that believeth in me shall never thirst.

---

of bread? They may be asking for (1) some *lasting* sign, like the daily gift of manna; (2) some sign from *heaven* (again like the manna, which they imagined fell from the sky: in Matt. 16: 1 and Mark 8: 11 a 'sign from Heaven' is asked for directly after the second multiplication of bread:) or (3) a sign which would warrant their giving to *Him* (σύ and σοί are emphatic) a trust similar to that which they gave to God.

31. The allusion is to Ps. 77: 29.

32. The contrast is triple: the Giver is not merely Moses, but God: the Bread is different in nature: Moses 'gave' (aorist), but 'My Father *is giving*—offering—you the True Bread' (present), which truly descends from heaven.

33. The words could signify: 'The bread of God is the bread that comes down from heaven and gives life to the world', or 'is He who etc.'

34. Exactly like the Samaritan Woman (4: 15) they choose the material alternative and ask to be always given such bread!

35. The doctrine moves forward step by step. Our Lord removes all ambiguity (not breaking off the discourse as He did with the Samaritaness): '*I am the Bread of Life*.' 'To come to Him' and 'to believe in Him' are equivalents. 'To come' does not mean mere bodily approach, any more than to 'see' or

36. But I said unto you that you also have seen me, and you believe not.

37. All that the Father giveth to me shall come to me: and him that cometh to me, I will not cast out.

38. Because I came down from heaven, not to do my own will but the will of him that sent me.

39. Now this is the will of the Father who sent me: that of all that he hath given me, I should lose nothing; but should raise it up again in the last day.

40. And this is the will of my Father that sent me: that every one who seeth the Son and believeth in him may have life everlasting. And I will raise him up in the last day.

41. The Jews therefore murmured at him, because he had said: I am the living bread which came down from heaven.

---

to 'hear' mean merely to look at or listen to with the ears. All these expressions mean an interior adhesion of mind, will and heart to our Lord. That after such 'adhesion' a man will no more hunger or thirst does not mean that after his first 'act of faith' a believer need take no more trouble, but no new *sort* of adhesion to Christ is required; the gift is a lasting gift, unless he throws it away (cf. 37, 39).

36. When was this said? If with some important MSS. we delete 'Me', there is a possible reference to 26: or, St John may allude to something he remembers but has not reported: finally, the verse may be out of place, and it would follow 40 better.

37-40. Our Lord stresses that it is through *Him* that we must reach the Father: *He* will not repel anyone who comes to Him: He has no purpose of His own, other than that of the Father, which is man's salvation.

40. He who thus sees and believes has already in him that 'Eternal Life' which bodily death cannot put an end to. (The reproach of verse 36 certainly fits better in here.)

41. 'About Him', rather than 'at Him'. The enthusiasm due to the miracle had already flagged: now there is frank hostility.

42. And they said: Is not this Jesus, the son of Joseph, whose father and mother we know? How then saith he: I came down from heaven?

43. Jesus therefore answered and said to them: Murmur not among yourselves.

44. No man can come to me, except the Father, who hath sent me, draw him. And I will raise him up in the last day.

45. It is written in the prophets: *And they shall all be taught of God.* Every one that hath heard of the Father and hath learned cometh to me.

46. Not that any man hath seen the Father: but he who is of God, he hath seen the Father.

47. Amen, amen, I say unto you: He that believeth in me hath everlasting life.

48. I am the bread of life.

---

42. 'This man' (οὗτος): almost 'this fellow'. The mention of Joseph does not suggest that he was alive: Jews were known in any case as sons of their *father*: but St John from beginning to end introduces our Lady by herself, without allusion to St Joseph.

43. Our Lord does not reply directly to their criticism, but emphasizes what He had been saying.

44, 45. No one can move towards Jesus if the Father do not draw him (Is. 54: 13; Jer. 31: 33, 34): but not all have listened and *learnt*: if they *have* learnt, it is to Jesus that they come.

46. No one has seen God, except Him who is 'along with' God, Jesus Himself. This is not the same affirmation as 1: 1; or 1: 18, where identity of nature is stated; our Lord here states that He is with God and sent from Him: see, still more clearly, 7: 29.

47. This sums up what has been affirmed so far—he who believes, on Christ's word, *has* Eternal life. But verse 48 repeats and will develop 35: and it is now that the Discourse becomes fully Eucharistic. Even the Jews could have understood that Christ claimed to be the nourishment of the soul by means of faith: He will now say that the bread He gives is actually His body and blood.

49. Your fathers did eat manna in the desert: and are dead.

50. This is the bread which cometh down from heaven: that if any man eat of it, he may not die.

51. I am the living bread which came down from heaven.

52. If any man eat of this bread, he shall live for ever; and the bread that I will give is my flesh, for the life of the world.

The Eucharistic Discourse (iii): 53–60

53. The Jews therefore strove among themselves, saying: How can this man give us his flesh to eat?

54. Then Jesus said to them: Amen, amen, I say unto you: except you eat the flesh of the Son of man and drink his blood, you shall not have life in you.

55. He that eateth my flesh and drinketh my blood hath everlasting life: and I will raise him up in the last day.

49, 50. Here is an echo of 31 ff. The material 'bread', the manna, did not save the Hebrews from physical death: this heavenly Bread *will* save those who feed on it from everlasting spiritual death.

51–52. Our Lord here takes everything over to the first person: 'I am the living Bread that came down from heaven'; the aorist verb may be contrasted with 'which is coming', translating the Greek present participle in 50; the divine gift—faith in Jesus and nourishment by Him—is endlessly recurrent: the Incarnation took place once and for all. 'My flesh for the life, etc.' means 'My flesh which is given for, etc.': the notion of sacrifice here enters along with that of the Eucharist.

53. The Jews 'fought *among themselves*'. About what point? Whether our Lord's words *could* be taken allegorically, or not? '*How* can . . .?' Cf. 3: 4.

54. Our Lord, as usual, emphasizes what He has said, not minimizing or turning it into metaphor, but using the word $\sigma \acute{\alpha} \rho \xi$, 'flesh', not 'body', and the word $\tau \rho \acute{\omega} \gamma \epsilon \iota \nu$ (54) instead of $\phi \alpha \gamma \epsilon \hat{\imath} \nu$ for 'eat', and putting His doctrine first

56. For my flesh is meat indeed: and my blood is drink indeed.

57. He that eateth my flesh and drinketh my blood abideth in me: and I in him.

58. As the living Father hath sent me and I live by the Father: so he that eateth me, the same also shall live by me.

59. This is the bread that came down from heaven. Not as your fathers did eat manna and are dead. He that eateth this bread shall live for ever.

60. These things he said, teaching in the synagogue, in Capharnaum.

---

negatively 'If you do not eat . . . you have not' and then positively: 'He that eateth . . . hath . . .' Ἀληθής 'real', is not quite the same as ἀληθινός; it forcibly excludes the idea of 'imaginary'.

57. Cf. John 4: 15; 5: 24; and in the Supper Room, 15: 4–7; 17: 23. St John's insistence on the truth that the divine Gift is not transitory, as though it were a passing emotion of our own: it incorporates us into Jesus, and, He makes His home in us. This does not prevent our wilfully, by sin, breaking off this union: still, we can say that in anyone in whom it has ever existed a sort of 'appetite' (even unconscious) for it survives;

58. it is not so hard to recover it as to create it. 'I live by, i.e. on account of the Father . . . so he who eateth Me shall live because of Me, i.e. owing to My "influx" into him' *may* be the true (and is the usual) rendering. But here the new idea of 'mission' comes in: 'As the Living Father sent Me, and I live for the sake of the Father, so he that eateth Me *shall* live for My sake': his life too will be a missionary, apostolic

59. life. This sums up and includes all that had been said before.

60. These things He said teaching in the synagogue, in Capharnaum. In the Greek there is no article; it is as though we said: 'in church', an official 'catechism'. Yet it is hard to suppose that our Lord made this very mystical discourse to all alike—to the average Galilean, surely unable to follow what He meant. There is at any rate a 'break' after verse 40. The subject of the Jews' 'murmuring' was not yet the Eucharist,

The Eucharistic Discourse (iv): 61–72

61. Many therefore of his disciples, hearing it, said: This saying is hard; and who can hear it?

62. But Jesus, knowing in himself that his disciples murmured at this, said to them: Doth this scandalize you?

63. If then you shall see the Son of man ascend up where he was before?

---

but the heavenly origin of our Lord. A second 'chapter', so to say, of doctrine follows, 43–52, in which our Lord re-affirms His divine mission, but says that *He* is the Bread from heaven, and that this Bread is His flesh. We must leave a space for the Jews' dispute (53), so that the last part may have been addressed primarily to His disciples, though in the synagogue. It may have been the place that gave His speech its solemnity, not some official occasion, like the sabbath. In any case, St John's readers cannot but have seen the Eucharist in this discourse, even though our Lord does not begin by speaking of it, and though the Eucharist itself is but the supreme means of entering forthwith into Eternal Life. True, in so far as the Eucharist *is* an incorporation in Christ, it can be regarded as an end: yet our eternal life of Communion is different from our recurrent sacramental Communions.

61. 'Hear it': possibly 'make sense of it': possibly they imagine that the actual flesh which they see is to be eaten, and retire in horror.

62, 63. This difficult phrase must mean: 'Does what I have said shock you? What then, should you see the Son of Man ascending to where He was before?' But what exactly does *that* mean? Cf. 1: 51; 3: 13 for the construction. Presumably, 'When you see me ascending to My true home heaven, you will understand that it is not this earthly flesh of Mine that you are to eat, as [St Augustine ruthlessly says] flesh is torn from a dead body or sold in the market, but My living Self, body, soul, spirit', and the whole point of the Eucharist is a spiritual union

64. It is the spirit that quickeneth: the flesh profiteth nothing. The words that I have spoken to you are spirit and life.

65. But there are some of you that believe not. For Jesus knew from the beginning who they were that did not believe and who he was that would betray him.

66. And he said: Therefore did I say to you that no man can come to me, unless it be given him by my Father.

67. After this, many of his disciples went back and walked no more with him.

68. Then Jesus said to the twelve: Will you also go away?

69. And Simon Peter answered him: Lord, to whom shall we go? Thou hast the words of eternal life.

70. And we have believed and have known that thou art the Christ, the Son of God.

71. Jesus answered them: Have not I chosen you twelve? And one of you is a devil.

---

with Himself. Anything *merely* 'flesh' would indeed profit nothing.

64. A parenthesis. St John does not want us to think that our Lord promised perseverance to all, even of those whom He had called, even to the traitor-to-be. He always knew, from the outset, who would be faithless.

66. 'From then on' rather than 'in consequence of' these last words, or of the whole discourse.

67. St John assumes that of course his readers know about the calling of the Twelve.

68–70. Peter answers in the name of all: they, at any rate, believe. We should read 'We know that Thou art the Holy One of God'. It cannot be said that he explicitly affirms the divinity of our Lord, nor yet that he is ignorant of it: he had as yet no 'theological' terms in which to express a faith that Christ was *God*. Some think this is the same as St Peter's confession in

71. Matt. 16: 16. Our Lord answers: 'Was it not *I* who chose you —the "Twelve"? Yet one of you is a devil!' This is different from our Lord's calling Peter 'Satan' ('Adversary'), Mark 8:

72. Now he meant Judas Iscariot, the son of Simon: for this same was about to betray him, whereas he was one of the twelve.

33; Matt. 16: 23), and again, from Luke 22: 3, where Satan is said to enter into Judas. Nor does it mean that Judas was 'possessed'. It really means that Judas has definitely turned against Him, or will so turn, and is playing the part of him who was pre-eminent in the spiritual world as Adversary.

CHAPTER SEVEN

Jesus goes to Jerusalem: 1–13

1. After these things, Jesus walked in Galilee: for he would not walk in Judea, because the Jews sought to kill him.
2. Now the Jews' feast of tabernacles was at hand.
3. And his brethren said to him: Pass from hence and go into Judea, that thy disciples also may see thy works which thou dost.

---

1. 'Walked': went to and fro: went about. Both St Mark (9: 30) and St Matthew (17: 21) show that our Lord spent a considerable time towards the end of His life in training His disciples: He did not go to Jerusalem because the Jews there wished to kill him (5: 18) for violating the sabbath, and since St John (verses 23 and following) shows Him defending His actions on the sabbath and referring to their intention of killing Him for His actions on that day, we see that this chapter does fit on to the end of Chapter 5 better than to Chapter 6. Anyhow 'after this' marks a considerable interval, perhaps six months: the Feast of Tents occurred about the end of September, as a harvest-thanksgiving, and also in memory of the time when the Hebrews lived in tents after leaving Egypt: cf. Ex. 23: 16; Lev. 23: 34–43. Quite recently, and perhaps still today, Jews in Palestine built huts which they adorned with branches, etc.: the feast was more popular than religious.

3. Our Lord's brethren (see on Mark 3: 31 etc.) urged Him to come to the festival and declare Himself. They did not fully believe in His spiritual claims, but they did not regard Him any more as a mere enthusiast: they recognized that He had worked many miracles in Galilee, but if He really had a

63

4. For there is no man that doth any thing in secret, and he himself seeketh to be known openly. If thou do these things, manifest thyself to the world.

5. For neither did his brethren believe in him.

6. Then Jesus said to them: My time is not yet come; but your time is always ready.

7. The world cannot hate you: but me it hateth, because I give testimony of it, that the works thereof are evil.

8. Go you up to this festival day: but I go not up to this festival day, because my time is not accomplished.

9. When he had said these things, he himself stayed in Galilee.

10. But after his brethren were gone up, then he also went up to the feast, not openly, but, as it were, in secret.

11. The Jews therefore sought him on the festival day and said: Where is he?

12. And there was much murmuring among the multitude concerning him. For some said: He is a good man. And others said: No, but he seduceth the people.

13. Yet no man spoke openly of him, for fear of the Jews.

---

message for everyone, He must seek publicity and not shut Himself up far away. Jerusalem was the proper place for that.

6. That is, 'this is not the moment for *me* to go to Jerusalem: *you* are free to do as you like'.

7. 'The world'; in particular the Jerusalem Jews (cf. verse 1). Our Lord's whole life and doctrine were a reproach to the 'world' of men like those Jews and indeed His brethren.

8. Here, 'moment' (καιρός) clearly means the hour for His decisive entry into Jerusalem.

9. He refrained therefore from a public entry into the City, especially as such pilgrimages took on an official, organized character as they neared it.

11, 12. Opinions about our Lord were mixed: the leading Jews were clearly hostile to Him; still, He was expected at the Feast.

Jesus teaches in the Temple: 14–24

14. Now, about the midst of the feast, Jesus went up into the temple and taught.

15. And the Jews wondered, saying: How doth this man know letters, having never learned?

16. Jesus answered them and said: My doctrine is not mine, but his that sent me.

17. If any man will do the will of him, he shall know of the doctrine, whether it be of God, or whether I speak of myself.

18. He that speaketh of himself seeketh his own glory: but he that seeketh the glory of him that sent him, he is true and there is no injustice in him.

19. Did not Moses give you the law, and *yet* none of you keepeth the law?

---

14. Not 'about', but 'already'. The feast was already half over: it lasted seven days, with one day added.

15. 'Letters' (γράμματα), different from γραφαί, the Scriptures, suggests an angry exaggeration. He had had no official instruction—'he can't so much as read!' His doctrine, therefore, must be 'his own': he is an innovator, subtly seducing the ignorant (cf. verses 12, 47).

16. 'Not *merely* Mine'; cf. 6: 27.

17. The Jews knew God's will through the Commandments: if they '*willed* to do *His* Will', there would come to exist an inclination to accept our Lord's teaching as what it really was: but alas, He is about to say, you do *not* keep the Command-

18. ments. A parenthesis. Unless a man be sent from God, he is sure to seek his own glorification: but our Lord is *not* doing this, and should be accepted as truthful (ἀληθής) and without fault.

19. 'Since none of you keep the Law, why seek to kill *Me*?' This looks back to 5: 18: now if Chapter 6 precedes Chapter 7, the events of Chapter 5 were over a year ago. But if Chapter 7 follows Chapter 5 an interval of only a month or two is

20. Why seek you to kill me? The multitude answered and said: Thou hast a devil. Who seeketh to kill thee?

21. Jesus answered and said to them: One work I have done: and you all wonder.

22. Therefore, Moses gave you circumcision (not because it is of Moses, but of the fathers): and on the sabbath day you circumcise a man.

23. If a man receive circumcision on the sabbath day, that the law of Moses may not be broken: are you angry at me, because I have healed the whole man on the sabbath day?

24. Judge not according to the appearance: but judge just judgment.

The Plan to Kill Our Lord: 25–30

25. Some therefore of Jerusalem said: Is not this he whom they seek to kill?

26. And behold, he speaketh openly: and they say nothing to him. Have the rulers known for a truth that this is the Christ?

---

20. implied. The crowd at any rate does not dream of their chiefs' wish to kill Jesus, and say that He must be more than crazy—must be possessed—if He imagines any such intention.

21. 'One work': this must apparently refer to the cure at Bethesda on the sabbath. Well—Moses ordained circumcision on the eighth day after birth (St John inserts a reminder that this rite dated from before Moses—Gen. 17: 12: it was presumably a hygienic practice common to many besides the Hebrews and preserved among them and made part of the Law by Moses), and, to keep his law, you perform it on the eighth day, sabbath or not (22): therefore, the Law about the sabbath has to make way for a ritual observance, relatively much less important: much more, then, must it yield in favour of the merciful cure of the whole of a man: cf. Mark 3: 4; and Matt. 12: 5.

24. Verdict should be passed, not merely on the concrete, material act, but on the moral intention with which it is done. (This is not saying that a good intention justifies an evil act. The cure of the sick man was *not* in itself wrong.)

27. But we know this man, whence he is: but when the Christ cometh, no man knoweth, whence he is.
28. Jesus therefore cried out in the temple, teaching and saying: You both know me, and you know whence I am. And I am not come of myself: but he that sent me is true, whom you know not.
29. I know him, because I am from him: and he hath sent me.
30. They sought therefore to apprehend him: and no man laid hands on him, because his hour was not yet come.

The Pharisees seek to arrest Him: 31-36

31. But of the people many believed in him and said: When the Christ cometh, shall he do more miracles than these which this man doth?
32. The Pharisees heard the people murmuring these things concerning him: and the rulers and Pharisees sent ministers to apprehend him.
33. Jesus therefore said to them: Yet a little while I am with you: and *then* I go to him that sent me.

---

26. Silence suggests approval. Yet 'surely the chiefs cannot have genuinely acknowledged . . .' μήποτε: cf. Latin *num*.
27. It was thought by many that the Messias would appear suddenly; but the origin and activity of Jesus in Galilee were known.
28. 'Yes, you know Me and My home; *yet* I have been *sent*, and He who sent Me is a "true", i.e. has the right to the name of, Sender (ἀληθής 'genuine' is different from ἀληθινός 'truth-speaking'), and *Him* you do not know.'
28. 'I know Him, because I come from Him, and it is *He* who has sent Me', cf. Matt. 11: 27. This claim to a unique existence along with God, before and during His earthly life, was understood by His hearers, who tried to seize Him, but he avoided them—St John does not say how.
32. For 'rulers' read 'chief priests' (cf. Acts 4: 6): why did the 'servants *not* arrest Him'? Presumably they waited for some 'word of blasphemy', but our Lord did not, at the moment, commit Himself further.
33. Possibly the 'little time' amounted to six months.

34. You shall seek me and shall not find me: and where I am, *thither* you cannot come.

35. The Jews therefore said among themselves: Whither will he go, that we shall not find him? Will he go unto the dispersed among the Gentiles and teach the Gentiles?

36. What is this saying that he hath said: You shall seek me and shall not find me? And: Where I am, you cannot come?

The Living Water: 37–44

37. And on the last, *and* great day of the festivity, Jesus stood and cried, saying: If any man thirst, let him come to me and drink.

38. He that believeth in me, as the scripture saith: *Out of his belly shall flow rivers of living water.*

---

34. Practically, 'should you seek Me, you would not find Me: you cannot even come to where I am': Jesus, as Son of God, is intangible. After He had left the world, and disasters befell the Jews, they would indeed try to find a Messias, but would fail.

35. The *diaspora* 'of the Greeks' meant Jews dispersed outside Palestine among 'Gentiles'. The Jews repeat all that He had said save the key-words—that He was returning to Him who sent Him.

37–38. This may be the seventh day of the Feast of Tabernacles, or the eighth, when the people left their huts and commemorated their entry into the Holy Land. During the week water was carried up in a gold vessel from the Pool of Siloe (9: 7) and poured out in memory of the water struck by Moses from the rock (Ex. 17: 6, etc.) while Is. 12: 3 and perhaps Ps. 104: 41 were sung. Either on the seventh day, then, our Lord 'cried aloud, standing up', 'Come to *Me*, and *I* will give you living water!' (cf. 4: 10), or, He did so when the ritual ceremonies were over: in either case, He marked the contrast. Either we put a full stop after 'he that believeth in me', and read: 'If a man thirst, let him come to Me, and let him who believes in

39. Now this he said of the Spirit which they should receive who believed in him: for as yet the Spirit was not given, because Jesus was not yet glorified.

40. Of that multitude therefore, when they had heard these words of his, some said: This is the prophet indeed.

41. Others said: This is the Christ. But some said: Doth the Christ come out of Galilee?

42. Doth not the scripture say: That Christ cometh of the seed of David and from Bethlehem the town where David was?

43. So there arose a dissension among the people because of him.

44. And some of them would have apprehended him: but no man laid hands upon him.

Me drink!' or, regard 'He who believes . . .' as a 'nominativus pendens', and continue: 'as the Scripture says, forth from his heart shall flow, etc.' This seems to be the normal punctuation in antiquity. The reference may be to Is. 48: 21; 58: 11; or to Zach. 14: 8. With the former punctuation, it is presumably from Jesus that the Spirit is to flow: with the second, the man who has drunk from Christ communicates his gift to others: he himself becomes a source. 'Bowels' (κοιλία) means the 'interior', the 'heart', as we would easily say; e.g. 'from the heart of the woods'. See Apoc. 21: 6: in Apoc. 22: 1, the River of Life is certainly the Holy Spirit.

39. A parenthesis by St John, explaining that this was a prophecy: Jesus was yet to be glorified (by His ascension), and then only would the Spirit be given, i.e. at Pentecost.

42. The point at issue is the Galilean origin of Jesus: Micheas 5: 2 had prophesied that the Messias should not only descend from David but come from David's town, Bethlehem: the birth of Jesus there had been an 'accident', due to the distant census: He was known as 'of Nazareth'.

43. Had any of the 'crowd' laid hold of Jesus, they would presumably have taken Him to the Sanhedrin, and hardly have dared to kill Him themselves.

Whence is the Christ?: 45–53

45. The ministers therefore came to the chief priests and the Pharisees. And they said to them: Why have you not brought him?
46. The ministers answered: Never did man speak like this man.
47. The Pharisees therefore answered them: Are you also seduced?
48. Hath any one of the rulers believed in him, or of the Pharisees?
49. But this multitude, that knoweth not the law, are accursed.
50. Nicodemus said to them (he that came to him by night, who was one of them):
51. Doth our law judge any man, unless it first hear him and know what he doth?
52. They answered and said to him: Art thou also a Galilean? Search the scriptures, and see that out of Galilee a prophet riseth not.
53. And every man returned to his own house.

---

45. Not only had the 'servants' not heard on *this* occasion anything 'blasphemous', but they had felt the difference in 'tone' between our Lord's preaching and anyone else's—noticeable from the outset (Matt. 7: 29; Mark 1: 22).

47–52. The violence of the language of the Pharisees indicated their anger. Not only must subordinates simply carry out orders and not have opinions of their own, but the populace ignores the Law and therefore is accursed.

50 ff. All the more exasperating was the intervention of Nicodemus, whose argument could not be refuted. Hence the arbitrary and escapist statement that no prophet (not 'has arisen', but) *arises* in, i.e. comes from Galilee, despite Jonas, (4 Kings, 14: 25).

CHAPTER EIGHT

The Woman taken in Adultery: 1–11

1. And Jesus went unto mount Olivet.
2. And early in the morning he came again into the temple: and all the people came to him. And sitting down he taught them.
3. And the scribes and Pharisees bring unto him a woman taken in adultery: and they set her in the midst,
4. And said to him: Master, this woman was even now taken in adultery.
5. Now Moses in the law commanded us to stone such a one. But what sayest thou?

It has been denied that this passage is genuine. It is lacking in many MSS.; where it occurs it is not always quoted in the same way; in one set of MSS. it occurs at the end of John, in another after Luke 21: 38. Practically all the Greek or oriental commentators ignore it; it is said to contain expressions not in St John's style (but we doubt if so short a passage suffices for forming a judgment). On the other hand, omissions are more frequently and more easily made than additions, and this passage may have been early omitted lest its doctrine should seem lax. The Council of Trent implies that the passage is inspired and canonical, but does not decide the authorship.

3. The Scribes are mentioned only here by St John.
4. For placing someone in the middle of a ring of onlookers cf. Luke 6: 8 (the man with the withered hand, etc.) 'in the act' ('ἐπ' αὐτοφώρῳ); not 'even now'. Lev. 20: 10 decrees death in the case of an adulterous wife; stoning, in that of an engaged young woman; but this law could not be carried out under Roman rule.

6. And this they said tempting him, that they might accuse him. But Jesus bowing himself down, wrote with his finger on the ground.

7. When therefore they continued asking him, he lifted up himself and said to them: He that is without sin among you, let him first cast a stone at her.

8. And again stooping down, he wrote on the ground.

9. But they hearing *this*, went out one by one, beginning at the eldest. And Jesus alone remained, and the woman standing in the midst.

10. Then Jesus lifting up himself, said to her: Woman, where are they that accused thee? Hath no man condemned thee?

11. Who said: No man, Lord. And Jesus said: Neither will I condemn thee. Go, and now sin no more.

The Light of the World: 12–20

12. Again therefore, Jesus spoke to them, saying: I am the light of the world. He that followeth me walketh not in darkness, but shall have the light of life.

---

6. Our Lord was not seated on a teacher's official chair, but on some low stool or cushion so that by leaning forward he could make marks on the earth. It signified a refusal to listen to the accusers, but we cannot tell what He wrote, if anything.

7. This does not mean that only a judge whose conscience is clear of grave sin can pronounce a just verdict, but He leaves them to their sense of shame. St John implies that the eldest would have had the most to reproach themselves with.

10. It does not follow that everyone else who had been present went away: but only the woman and our Lord play the decisive role.

11. Our Lord did not say that her sin had been no sin, but that He did not condemn her as deserving of the threatened punishment, or as still guilty in God's sight. 'Sin no more' implies both contrition and resolution for the future.

12. Jesus spoke what follows in the 'treasury' (20) which was in the court of the women. Now in the night of the first to the

13. The Pharisees therefore said to him: Thou givest testimony of thyself. Thy testimony is not true.

14. Jesus answered and said to them: Although I give testimony of myself, my testimony is true: for I know whence I came and whither I go. But you know not whence I come or whither I go.

15. You judge according to the flesh: I judge not any man.

16. And if I do judge, my judgment is true: because I am not alone, but I and the Father that sent me.

---

second day of the feast just over, two candelabra were lit there, commemorating the Pillar of Fire in Ex. 13: 21, 22, and supposed to illuminate all Palestine. It can hardly be doubted that our Lord, saying '*I* am the Light of the *World*' both alluded to this and lifted its meaning to a sublime level; besides, the Hebrews had been accustomed to the comparison of the Messias with light, and the N.T. had used such prophecies: see Matt. 4: 14 ff. and Is. 9: 1, 2: and Simeon in Luke 2: 32 and Is. 42: 6; 49: 6. Here the faithful disciple 'walks' in the light shed by our Lord: in Matt. 5: 14, He says: '*You* are the light of the world!' rather as above (7: 38) the Faithful transmit the Living Water they receive. Cf. 3: 21; 12: 35, 36, 46; 1 John 1: 5–7.

14. Our Lord had allowed that no man is 'witness in his own cause' (5: 31), but He appeals to Himself as sent by God, as His 'works' prove (5: 36), and also to His personal knowledge of His origin and destiny (the Ascension): this could not be understood by the Jews in the full sense in which we can: but from what they had seen, they should have known He was more than He seemed to the outward eye, a man like other men, no more.

15. 'Judge' ($K\rho\acute{\iota}\nu\epsilon\iota\nu$) is practically as in 7: 24. Our Lord says He judges no man (cf. 3: 17; 12: 47), because it was not His function during His earthly life of salvation, to condemn: He contrasts this with the Pharisees who were obstinately condemning Him, and shutting evidence out.

16–18. Yet 'even if I *did* judge', that judgment would be valid,

SAINT JOHN

17. And in your law it is written that the testimony of two men is true.
18. I am one that give testimony of myself: and the Father that sent me giveth testimony of me.
19. They said therefore to him: Where is thy Father? Jesus answered: Neither me do you know, nor my Father. If you did know me, perhaps you would know my Father also.
20. These words Jesus spoke in the treasury, teaching in the temple: and no man laid hands on him, because his hour was not yet come.

God is the Father: 21–30

21. Again therefore Jesus said to them: I go: and you shall seek me. And you shall die in your sin. Whither I go, you cannot come.
22. The Jews therefore said: Will he kill himself, because he said: Whither I go, you cannot come?

---

because it would be the joint judgment pronounced by Himself and His Father—the two witnesses exacted by the Law (Dt. 19: 15). But this could not have impressed His hearers, for they would have seen in our Lord just a man giving witness to himself, and as for his 'father', they did not see him at all, but forthwith asked: 'Where is he?'

19. Our Lord replies that if they had understood *Him*, they would have realized that He had always identified 'Him who had sent Him', 'His Father', and God.
20. 'The treasury' must mean the place where gifts were offered (Luke 21: 1, 2) which was in the Court of the Women.
21. Possibly this is a detached discourse: verse 20 suggests an interruption; and what follows is very like 7: 31–36: our Lord reiterates, with emphasis (as He often did), something already taught. He assumes that their ill-will is fixed: they are, and will be, responsible for their doom (cf. Dt. 24: 16: also Ezech. 3: 19; 18: 24).
22. The question is surely ironic: 'Will he take the only way of escaping us—suicide?' They can hardly be recalling that the fate of a suicide was Gehenna, for our Lord did not say: 'You

74

23. And he said to them: You are from beneath: I am from above. You are of this world: I am not of this world.

24. Therefore I said to you that you shall die in your sins. For if you believe not that I am he, you shall die in your sin.

25. They said therefore to him: Who art thou? Jesus said to them: The beginning, who also speak unto you.

26. Many things I have to speak and to judge of you. But he that sent me, is true: and the things I have heard of him, these same I speak in the world.

---

will not come', but 'you *cannot* come'. Anyhow He disregards the suggestion and proceeds to say that He is from 'above', super-mundane: *they* are as it were rooted in the lower worldly life. Still, a door of hope *is* opened—'If you believe' . . . But believe what? 'That I am . . .' the Vulgate adds 'He': If our Lord was claiming the ancient Name of God: 'I am who am' (Ex. 3: 14), the Jews would have been horror-struck as we see them to be in verse 58. It must mean 'He whom you expect, or hope for': our Lord does not directly use the name 'Messias', as too much involved in materialist hopes.

25. They ask, therefore, *who* He is. His answer is very obscure. In the Latin, 'principium qui et loquor vobis' is a literal translation and can hardly mean anything save 'The Origin, who am in fact speaking to you': but this does not account for the accusative τὴν ἀρχήν and *qui* is not in the Greek. The Greek Fathers on the whole take τὴν ἄρχήν as a conjunction, and make the sentence into an exclamation of disgust at having to talk with men so slow to understand. Thus we could translate: 'To start with, that I should speak with you (at all)!' or, taking τὴν ἀρχήν in the sense of ὅλως, which really means the same: 'That I should talk with you at all! (cf.

26. (Luke 9: 41) (*But*) I have much more to say about you, (*yet*) I will say only what I have heard from Him who sent Me, and what I say will be truthful, because *He* is truthful.'

75

27. And they understood not that he called God his Father.

28. Jesus therefore said to them: When you shall have lifted up the Son of man, then shall you know that I am he and that I do nothing of myself. But as the Father hath taught me, these things I speak.

29. And he that sent me is with me: and he hath not left me alone. For I do always the things that please him.

30. When he spoke these things, many believed in him.

'The Seed of Abraham': 31-38

31. Then Jesus said to those Jews who believed him: If you continue in my word, you shall be my disciples indeed.

32. And you shall know the truth: and the truth shall make you free.

33. They answered him: We are the seed of Abraham: and we have never been slaves to any man. How sayest thou: You shall be free?

---

27. They did not grasp that He was speaking to them of the Father (not, 'that God was His father'). But in verse 18 His listeners *had* understood it? We assume, then, that the present audience was different.

28. When they shall have lifted Him high on the Cross, and the subsequent disasters began to befall them, they would realize that His mission had indeed been from God.

29. The Father, for His part, sends His Son, and the Son, on His side, does nothing save what pleases His Father.

30. They 'believed', but with no lasting or deep adhesion to our Lord.

31, 32. 'Continue in' (John's favourite words, 'remain') means more than 'keep the amount of knowledge you now have'; it means to live in and by it: cf. 2 John verse 9: and 1 John 2: 6, 24, 27, etc. The *practice* of the truth (cf. 3: 21) leads to greater freedom.

33. Is this an extreme example of our Lord's hearers taking the material meaning of His words (3: 4; 4: 11, etc.)? How could they forget their enslavement under the Egyptians, Babylonians, etc., up to Antiochus Epiphanes? They must have meant that they had retained their spiritual liberty.

34. Jesus answered them: Amen, amen, I say unto you that whosoever committeth sin is the servant of sin.

35. Now the servant abideth not in the house for ever: but the son abideth for ever.

36. If therefore the son shall make you free, you shall be free indeed.

37. I know that you are the children of Abraham: but you seek to kill me, because my word hath no place in you.

38. I speak that which I have seen with my Father: and you do the things that you have seen with your father.

'Abraham is our Father': 39–47

39. They answered and said to him: Abraham is our father. Jesus saith to them: If you be the children of Abraham, do the works of Abraham.

40. But now you seek to kill me, a man who have spoken the truth to you, which I have heard of God. This Abraham did not.

41. You do the works of your father. They said therefore to him: We are not born of fornication: we have one Father, *even* God.

---

34. Yet, they had sinned: they needed a still deeper liberation.

35. The slave of sin could be expelled from his paternal home: the Son alone, who never leaves His Father, can set men free from sin.

37. Certainly they are descendants of Abraham; yet they try to kill Him! 'You seek to kill me'; 'you' must mean, not these semi-believers, but the chiefs and representatives of the Jews. In verse 44 He will say openly that their 'father' is the devil: here it is on His own Sonship that He insists.

39. They obstinately claim Abraham as father, and our Lord tells them to act as he would have acted:

40. 'but as it is,' (you are far from doing so), you seek to kill me.

41. He still does not say expressly, 'of the devil'. The Jews shift their ground; they see that our Lord accepts their physical descent from Abraham, and say: 'We are not illegitimate: we have one father—God!' The point is (apart from the innuendo

42. Jesus therefore said to them: If God were your Father, you would indeed love me. For from God I proceeded and came. For I came not of myself: but he sent me.

43. Why do you not know my speech? Because you cannot hear my word.

44. You are of *your* father the devil: and the desires of your father you will do. He was a murderer from the beginning: and he stood not in the truth, because truth is not in him. When he speaketh a lie, he speaketh of his own: for he is a liar, and the father thereof.

45. But if I say the truth, you believe me not.

46. Which of you shall convince me of sin? If I say the truth to you, why do you not believe me?

---

that Christ is *not* legitimate) that they have kept the true faith in One God: idolatry, polytheism, was constantly described as wantoning away from God (e.g. Osee, 1: 2; 2: 4).

43. 'Why (though I speak in terms familiar to you) do you not understand what I say? Because you cannot give heed to My doctrine.' They cannot, because they obstinately will not.

44. 'You will to do', not 'will do'. The devil has his *will* in regard of men, and that is what these Jews are intent on carrying out. 'From the beginning'; not that he was created evil, but from the beginning of his relations with mankind he wished to destroy their (spiritual) life: Wisdom 2: 24: 'By the envy (φθόνῳ), grudge, malice of the devil Death entered the world': see also Rom. 5: 12 ff. The devil had no foothold (ἔστηκεν) in the truth; he had become the Lie-in-the-concrete, so to say. All that issues from him is Lie.

45. 'But *I*, just because I tell you the truth, you do not believe Me': their minds had identified themselves with the mind of the Liar.

46. Suddenly He asks which of them can *convict* Him of sin? Were He lying, He *would* be sinning. 'Why do you not believe?' shows that the audience had not been, all the time,

47. He that is of God heareth the words of God. Therefore you hear them not, because you are not of God.

'Before Abraham was, I AM': 48–59

48. The Jews therefore answered and said to him: Do not we say well that thou art a Samaritan and hast a devil?

49. Jesus answered: I have not a devil: but I honour my Father. And you have dishonoured me.

50. But I seek not my own glory: there is one that seeketh and judgeth.

51. Amen, amen, I say to you: If any man keep my word, he shall not see death for ever.

---

the new 'believers'. We must picture a crowd, now larger, now smaller; impressed, or hostile. St John often neglects the *mise-en-scène* while his mind is intent on remembering the Lord's words.

47. These terrible words declare that His hearers did not have God for Father (as they had claimed): He was their Creator, but their soul had turned away from Him (cf. 1 John 4: 4, 6: and Matt. 23: 15; Mark 12: 6).

48. The increasing sternness of our Lord's words provoke the Jews to fury. Cf. 4: 9 for the hatred between Jews and Samaritans, and cf. Luke 10: 33. This was as bad as being possessed by a devil (not *the* devil), i.e. mad.

49. Our Lord disregards the taunt of 'Samaritan'; we do not read that the Jews had called Him this before, but they do now ('say', not 'said').

50. The 'I' ($\dot{\epsilon}\gamma\dot{\omega}$) is emphatic, as in the previous verse where it is contrasted with 'you': our Lord almost 'apologizes' for seeming to defend Himself: *God* is seeking His Son's glory and 'is judging' ($\kappa\rho\dot{\iota}\nu\omega\nu$); is deciding in His favour and so, condemning them.

51. He seems to soften this somewhat: 'If anyone is true to My word'—i.e. some will be, and shall have 'eternal life'.

52. The Jews therefore said: Now we know that thou hast a devil. Abraham is dead, and the prophets; and thou sayest: If any man keep my word, he shall not taste death for ever.

53. Art thou greater than our father Abraham who is dead? And the prophets are dead. Whom dost thou make thyself?

54. Jesus answered: If I glorify myself, my glory is nothing. It is my Father that glorifieth me, of whom you say that he is your God.

55. And you have not known him: but I know him. And if I shall say that I know him not, I shall be like to you, a liar. But I do know him and do keep his word.

56. Abraham your father rejoiced that he might see my day: he saw it and was glad.

57. The Jews therefore said to him: Thou art not yet fifty years old. And hast thou seen Abraham?

---

52. Again they take this in the material sense, since Abraham and the prophets are dead,

53. 'who do you profess to be?' Yet all that precedes made it clear that our Lord claimed a unique position, and even nature.

54, 55. The 'glory' due to and destined for the Son is gradually replacing the idea of 'witnessing to' Him; 11: 4; 12: 16, 23, 28 and in the final Discourse.

56. 'My day': not to be tied down to any particular event in our Lord's life, or to His death: still less to the sacrifice of Isaac interpreted mystically (Gen. 22: 1–18): nor do we think it refers to any special knowledge of the actual Incarnation acquired by Abraham in Limbo; but, to the great Act of Faith that he made in the promises of God and the blessing that was to come to and through his descendants; he believed stubbornly 'as though he saw what is invisible' (Hebr. 11: 27, of Moses): 'that (ἵνα) he might see' is not here 'final', but equivalent to 'in the hopes of, the assurance of, seeing My day', i.e. Me and My beneficent work.

57. It would have been more logical to say: 'You are not fifty years old—and did Abraham (dead long ago) see you?' But the point is, how could Abraham and Jesus have seen one

58. Jesus said to them: Amen, amen, I say to you, before Abraham was made, I AM.

59. They took up stones therefore to cast at him. But Jesus hid himself and went out of the temple.

---

another? ('Fifty years old' can have no reference to our Lord's exact age: 'even one half-century old!' is all that is meant.)

58. 'Before Abraham came into existence, *I am*': this is more than 'I *was*', for it is the Name of God and contrasts essential existence with coming to exist: cf. 1: 1, 2, 15, 30.

59. This will have sounded to a Jew as an obvious blasphemy and deserved stoning, Lev. 24: 16.

CHAPTER NINE

The Man born Blind: 1–12

1. And Jesus passing by, saw a man who was blind from his birth.
2. And his disciples asked him: Rabbi, who hath sinned, this man or his parents, that he should be born blind?
3. Jesus answered: Neither hath this man sinned, nor his parents; but that the works of God should be made manifest in him.
4. I must work the works of him that sent me, whilst it is day: the night cometh, when no man can work.
5. As long as I am in the world, I am the light of the world.
6. When he had said these things, he spat on the ground and made clay of the spittle and spread the clay upon his eyes,
7. And said to him: Go, wash in the pool of Siloe, which is interpreted, Sent. He went therefore and washed: and he came seeing.

---

2. The disciples did not allude to sin in some 'earlier incarnation', but simply yielded to the idea that all pain is punishment. Who had deserved it? The unborn child? The parents, then? 'That' here and in verse 3 is consecutive: there was no question of sin; but the result of his blindness was the manifestation of God's power in him.
4. Many MSS. have 'we' instead of 'I': cf. Matt. 3: 15: Jesus associates others (the disciples: the Baptist) with Himself and His work. For none of us does the 'day' last for ever.
5. So long as our Lord's earthly life lasted, He was Light of the World in a special way: He may have said this in the hearing of the blind man. For the use of saliva cf. Mark 7: 33; 8: 23. This would seem to have made the man still more blind besides being explicitly forbidden on the sabbath.
7. The word Siloah was applied rather to the channel bringing

8. The neighbours, therefore, and they who had seen him before that he was a beggar, said: Is not this he that sat and begged? Some said: This is he.

9. But others *said:* No, but he is like him. But he said: I am he.

10. They said therefore to him: How were thy eyes opened?

11. He answered: That man that is called Jesus made clay and anointed my eyes and said to me: Go to the pool of Siloe and wash. And I went: I washed: and I see.

12. And they said to him: Where is he? He saith: I know not.

The Pharisees examine the Man born Blind: 13–34

13. They bring him that had been blind to the Pharisees.

14. Now it was the sabbath, when Jesus made the clay and opened his eyes.

15. Again therefore the Pharisees asked him how he had received his sight. But he said to them: He put clay upon my eyes: and I washed: and I see.

16. Some therefore of the Pharisees said: This man is not of God, who keepeth not the sabbath. But others said: How can a man that is a sinner do such miracles? And there was a division among them.

17. They say therefore to the blind man again: What sayest thou of him that hath opened thy eyes? And he said: He is a prophet.

---

the water to the pool (still to be seen), and may mean 'Sender': St John adapts it so as to mean 'Sent'.

The story, told with extreme rapidity, says nothing of the emotions aroused by the miracle in the man himself or his circle: they may have remained almost stunned by the suddenness of so undreamed-of an event.

13. 'They'. Who? Clearly not his parents, who wished to keep out of the matter. People, then, who wished to learn the view of the chiefs of the national religion.

15. 'Again': i.e. others, though not the Pharisees, had questioned him.

17. Notice the popular use of 'prophet', not meaning one who *predicts*.

18. The Jews then did not believe concerning him, that he had been blind and had received his sight, until they called the parents of him that had received his sight,

19. And asked them, saying: Is this your son, who you say was born blind? How then doth he now see?

20. His parents answered them and said: We know that this is our son and that he was born blind:

21. But how he now seeth, we know not; or who hath opened his eyes, we know not. Ask himself: he is of age. Let him speak for himself.

22. These things his parents said, because they feared the Jews: for the Jews had already agreed among themselves that if any man should confess him to be Christ, he should be put out of the synagogue.

23. Therefore did his parents say: He is of age. Ask himself.

24. They therefore called the man again that had been blind and said to him: Give glory to God. We know that this man is a sinner.

25. He said therefore to them: If he be a sinner, I know not. One thing I know, that whereas I was blind, now I see.

26. They said then to him: What did he to thee? How did he open thy eyes?

27. He answered them: I have told you already, and you have heard. Why would you hear it again? Will you also become his disciples?

28. They reviled him therefore and said: Be thou his disciple; but we are the disciples of Moses.

29. We know that God spoke to Moses: but as to this man, we know not from whence he is.

30. The man answered and said to them: Why, herein is a wonderful thing, that you know not from whence he is, and he hath opened my eyes.

31. Now we know that God doth not hear sinners: but if a man be a server of God and doth his will, him he heareth.

---

22. Exclusion from the synagogue had long been a penalty: and cf. Luke 6: 22; John 12: 42; 16: 2.

24. 'Give glory to God' was a formula meaning: 'Tell the truth!'

27. The Pharisees could not but take this for an impertinence, and they sink to 'answering back'.

32. From the beginning of the world it hath not been heard, that any man hath opened the eyes of one born blind.

33. Unless this man were of God, he could not do any thing.

34. They answered and said to him: Thou wast wholly born in sins; and dost thou teach us? And they cast him out.

He worships Jesus: 35–41

35. Jesus heard that they had cast him out. And when he had found him, he said to him: Dost thou believe in the Son of God?

36. He answered, and said: Who is he, Lord, that I may believe in him?

37. And Jesus said to him: Thou hast both seen him; and it is he that talketh with thee.

38. And he said: I believe, Lord. And falling down, he adored him.

39. And Jesus said: For judgment I am come into this world; that they who see not may see; and they who see may become blind.

40. And some of the Pharisees, who were with him, heard: and they said unto him: Are we also blind?

---

34. Unnecessary to suppose they expressed a view as to the sinful origin of his blindness: they were in a rage, insulted him, and turned him out.

35. Our Lord *seeks* the man whom the others had cast out. Some chief MSS. have 'Son of Man': our Lord may have led him gently forward to a point where he would be able to *worship*.

37. 'and He that is speaking with thee—it is He!': ἐκεῖνός ἐστιν at the end is very emphatic.

38. The man's spiritual eyes, too, are definitely opened: he adores.

39. 'For judgment' (κρίνειν) (cf. 3: 17, etc.) here means 'to make a separation', cf. Luke 2: 34. As it were in spite of Himself, there are those who choose *against* Him. Things hidden from those who imagine they are wise, are revealed to simpler souls (cf. Matt. 11: 25; Luke 10: 21).

40. 'Surely *we* are not blind?' (μὴ καί: Latin: *num.*).

41. Jesus said to them: If you were blind, you should not have sin: but now you say: We see. Your sin remaineth.

---

41. If the Pharisees were blind as simple people are, and asked for enlightenment, that would be better than to be blind yet say that they *do* see, and to shut their eyes to the Light. That was wilful ignorance, and so long as it lasted, so did their sin.

This chapter is one supreme example of St John's power of writing a vivid story; of his deep irony; and of his seeing the spiritual 'bearing' of the historical events.

CHAPTER TEN

The Good Shepherd: 1–6

1. Amen, amen, I say to you: He that entereth not by the door into the sheepfold but climbeth up another way, the same is a thief and a robber.
2. But he that entereth in by the door is the shepherd of the sheep.
3. To him the porter openeth: and the sheep hear his voice. And he calleth his own sheep by name and leadeth them out.
4. And when he hath let out his own sheep, he goeth before them: and the sheep follow him, because they know his voice.
5. But a stranger they follow not, but fly from him, because they know not the voice of strangers.

---

1. We do not think there is any link between the paragraphs on the Shepherd and Chapter 9. 'Amen, amen' indicates at least a break in a discourse. The allusion in verse 21 may be due to St John's having recently *written* about the cure of the blind man, not to the cure having *happened* recently. We think verses 1–6 are an introduction to what follows and do not yet demand an interpretation. Thus the 'porter', gate-keeper, does not reappear. Picture an enclosure made of stakes and brambles, with a gate, containing sheep belonging to various shepherds. A thief may scramble over the enclosure, but the keeper opens the gate to a legitimate shepherd, who calls his own sheep by name (as is still done in Palestine) or by
2–5. playing a special tune on a pipe: he brings his own flock out and precedes them and they follow, he still playing or calling them: if they hear an alien call, they scamper away.

6. This proverb Jesus spoke to them. But they understood not what he spoke to them.

The Door of the Sheep: 7–10

7. Jesus therefore said to them again: Amen, amen, I say to you, I am the door of the sheep.

8. All *others*, as many as have come, are thieves and robbers: and the sheep heard them not.

9. I am the door. By me, if any man enter in, he shall be saved: and he shall go in and go out, and shall find pastures.

10. The thief cometh not, but for to steal and to kill and to destroy. I am come that they may have life and may have it more abundantly.

---

6. His hearers did not see any special point in this; and indeed it is but an introductory 'picture' or *mise-en-scène*.

7. A separate 'parable': as if our Lord said: 'So far as the *door* goes, it is Myself' (cf. 14: 6: 'no man cometh to the Father save by Me'). In the past, Moses and the Prophets were leading up to Him: in the future, there would be those who would shepherd the sheep, but succeed only in so far as they did it in His name, i.e. in His person.

9. 'Saved': no allusion to salvation: 'shall be safe and sound': no one will rebuke him. Nor does this allude to the sheep, who do not enter *save* by the door: it refers therefore to other 'shepherds' whom He will associate to Himself: 'to go in and go out' is a traditional phrase: cf. especially Num. 27: 17, where the leaders of the people shall come in and go out, and lead the people out and home again, so that the 'synagogue', i.e. assembly of the Lord shall not be like sheep that have no shepherd. Nor is the sheepfold, here, an image of the Church, for the shepherds go *out* to find pasturage. Cf. especially Ezech. 34.

8–10. Who are the 'thieves and brigands'? Such men wish to steal the sheep to eat or sell them, not merely to destroy them. Clearly not all who have come ('before Me' is rightly omitted) were destructive, e.g. Moses and the Prophets. Our

The Good Shepherd and the Hireling: 11–21

11. I am the good shepherd. The good shepherd giveth his life for his sheep.
12. But the hireling and he that is not the shepherd, whose own the sheep are not, seeth the wolf coming and leaveth the sheep and flieth: and the wolf catcheth and scattereth the sheep.
13. And the hireling flieth, because he is a hireling: and he hath no care for the sheep.
14. I am the good shepherd: and I know mine, and mine know me.
15. As the Father knoweth me, and I know the Father: and I lay down my life for my sheep.

Lord must mean those who come claiming, in some sense, a divine mission but *acted* as 'ravening wolves'; cf. Matt. 7: 15; 23: 14; Luke 11: 39, 52, among whom Our Lord would have placed the mass of scribes and Pharisees.

10. *He* had come (cf. Matt. 5: 17; 9: 13; and often in John) to give more life, not less. Can we think there is *only* a contrast here between Himself and the 'robbers'? We cannot but catch the 'overtones' of His words, and see a reference to the 'Eternal Life' of supernatural Grace, freely given, which is the essential theme of St John's gospel. This verse makes the transition to the new 'parable' of the Good Shepherd.

11. The description of kings, and David in particular, as shepherds, is frequent in the O.T.; n.b. Ezech. 34: 23; and see Matt. 18: 11–14; Luke 15: 3–7; our Lord is to be shepherd too of the 'scattered' people of Israel (Matt. 9: 36; 10: 6, 16; 15: 24), and as shepherd He is also Judge (Matt. 25: 32 ff.). The title is certainly Messianic; but here καλός, 'good', is almost 'genuine': not 'kindly': He offers (St John uses τιθέναι, 'lay down' where the Synoptists write δοῦναι 'give') His very life for the sheep.

12, 13. The hired man and the wolf do not indicate any definite persons: they serve to enhance the role of the true shepherd.

14, 15. True disciples know Him and are known by Him as He and the Father know one another.

16. And other sheep I have that are not of this fold: them also I must bring. And they shall hear my voice: and there shall be one fold and one shepherd.

17. Therefore doth the Father love me: because I lay down my life, that I may take it again.

18. No man taketh it away from me; but I lay it down of myself. And I have power to lay it down: and I have power to take it up again. This commandment have I received of my Father.

19. A dissension rose again among the Jews for these words.

20. And many of them said: He hath a devil and is mad. Why hear you him?

21. Others said: These are not the words of one that hath a devil. Can a devil open the eyes of the blind?

---

16. 'This fold' must be chosen people of Israel: there was no other fold: our Lord foresees that from these will come some whom too He will lead (not 'bring') so that there will come to be 'one flock, one shepherd'. It is a pity we have no English words to reproduce the echoing words ποίμνη, ποιμήν: once there *is* but a single flock under a single shepherd, it follows that there will come to be a single fold. The oneness of the Church is taken for granted, rather than proclaimed.

17, 18. 'Therefore' means: 'For this reason does My Father love Me—that I offer My life. 'That' (ὅτι) does not mean 'in order that', but a subsequent fact. In obedience to His Father's decree, He offers His life, but does so freely. He is glad to obey. There is a circle, as of knowledge, so of love between Him and His Father. And it is because of His divine nature that He can take up again the life that in His humanity He lays down.

19. 'Again': referring to 7: 43 rather than to 9: 16.

21. Not only the miracle has impressed them, but His words—not those of a madman!

'*I and the Father are ONE*': 22–30

22. And it was the feast of the dedication at Jerusalem: and it was winter.

23. And Jesus walked in the temple, in Solomon's porch.

24. The Jews therefore came round about him and said to him: How long dost thou hold our souls in suspense? If thou be the Christ, tell us plainly.

25. Jesus answered them: I speak to you, and you believe not: the works that I do in the name of my Father, they give testimony of me.

26. But you do not believe, because you are not of my sheep.

27. My sheep hear my voice. And I know them: and they follow me.

28. And I give them life everlasting: and they shall not perish for ever. And no man shall pluck them out of my hand.

29. That which my Father hath given me is greater than all: and no one can snatch *them* out of the hand of my Father.

---

22. The feast of the Dedication (or re-consecration of the temple and altar after their desecration by Antiochus Epiphanes) occurred in December, and lasted eight days. It does not seem necessary to suppose that everything since 7: 1 happened during the Feast of Tabernacles in September, and the discourse about the Shepherd (which seems almost to be continued here) may have been made much later in the autumn. Or St John may have inserted into this discussion phrases still in his mind from what he had just written.

23. The colonnade of Solomon, on the east of the Temple demesne, will have sheltered them from the colder winds.

24. 'Lift (our hopes) up' αἴρειν, and then leave them as it were hanging in mid-air. Jesus had not claimed publicly to be the Messias, which is what they wanted of Him.

26–29. If, after the miracles, they do not believe, it is because they *will* not: they exclude themselves from the flock. But those who do hear His voice have put themselves 'in His hand—His keeping', and no one can snatch them from His hand, any more than they can snatch anything from His Father's hand— for, He and the Father are *one thing* (ἕν). The thread of the

30. I and the Father are ONE.

The Jews seek to take our Lord again: 31–42

31. The Jews then took up stones to stone him.

32. Jesus answered them: Many good works I have shewed you from my Father. For which of those works do you stone me?

33. The Jews answered him: For a good work we stone thee not, but for blasphemy; and because that thou, being a man, makest thyself God.

34. Jesus answered them: Is it not written in your law: *I said, you are gods?*

35. If he called them gods to whom the word of God was spoken; and the scripture cannot be broken:

---

thought is clear; but verse 29 is not. There are two versions: 'The Father who has given Me (the sheep) is greater than all': Πατήρ, ὅς . . . μείζων. But the easier reading is always suspect; and the paramountcy of God was not in dispute. But also, 'The Father—what He has given Me is greater than all': Πατήρ, ὅ . . . μεῖζον: that is, the gift of the sheep—the salvation of souls—is more precious than anything else (apart, of course, from Our Lord's eternal Sonship), and the Father and the Son alike have them in their keeping.

30. That the Person of the Son is not that of the Father is indicated by the plural 'are' (ἐσμέν): but the neuter 'one' (ἕν) cannot but indicate that they are one in substance, in Godhead, not merely in power.

31. 'Again' (πάλιν), not 'then'. It seems disconcerting that men about to stone another should suddenly find their fury die out, and embark on an argument. But Orientalists assure us that that is what constantly happens.

34. From Ps. 81: 6, where magistrates are metaphorically (perhaps ironically) called 'gods' as *representing* the divine authority. Cf. Ex. 7: 1. The Scriptures as a whole could be called God's 'law':

36. Do you say of him whom the Father hath sanctified and sent into the world: Thou blasphemest; because I said: I am the Son of God?
37. If I do not the works of my Father, believe me not.
38. But if I do, though you will not believe me, believe the works: that you may know and believe that the Father is in me and I in the Father.
39. They sought therefore to take him: and he escaped out of their hands.
40. And he went again beyond the Jordan, into that place where John was baptizing first. And there he abode.
41. And many resorted to him: and they said: John indeed did no sign.
42. But all things whatsoever John said of this man were true. And many believed in him.

---

35. 'those to whom the word of God came' does not refer to the magistrates in question, but to all for whom the Scripture was inspired.
36. Our Lord does not conclude: 'Therefore I too can be meta-phorically called God', but insists anew that He is the Son of God, dedicated and sent by God, and that His works prove it. But verse 38 carries the matter once more to so high a point—the Father is *in* Him, and He *in* the Father—that the attack is renewed: our Lord escapes, maybe miraculously: this is not stated.
40. Before the climax of His ministry, our Lord retires to where it started: it was an interval of peace.

CHAPTER ELEVEN

The Raising of Lazarus (i): 1–16

1. Now there was a certain man sick, named Lazarus of Bethania, of the town of Mary and of Martha her sister.
2. (And Mary was she that anointed the Lord with ointment and wiped his feet with her hair: whose brother Lazarus was sick.)
3. His sisters therefore sent to him, saying: Lord, behold, he whom thou lovest is sick.
4. And Jesus hearing it, said to them: This sickness is not unto death, but for the glory of God: that the Son of God may be glorified by it.
5. Now Jesus loved Martha and her sister Mary and Lazarus.
6. When he had heard therefore that he was sick, he still remained in the same place two days.

---

1. Martha and Mary; cf. Luke 10: 38, 39. 'Lazarus' is probably for Eleazar: Bethany was on the east slope of Mount Olivet, about 15 furlongs from Jerusalem; cf. verse 18.
2. Ancient writers (save Origen) do not identify this Mary with the sinful woman who anointed our Lord in Luke 7: 38. Matt. 26: 6–13; Mark 14: 3–9, describe an anointing on the head, not feet: to us it seems more likely that it refers to John 12: 3.
3. They simply state the fact: cf. 2: 3: they could trust His love (verse 5).
4. This reply will have been taken to mean: 'Lazarus will not die'; but if it had been reported to the sisters, the shock might have been too great when he *did* die. We think it was spoken to the disciples, and meant at least a hint ($\pi\rho\dot{o}s$ $\theta\acute{a}\nu\alpha\tau o\nu$, cf. 1 John 5: 16, 17) that death was not to be the upshot of the episode, but the glory of God and glorification of His Son.

94

7. Then after that, he said to his disciples: Let us go into Judea again.

8. The disciples say to him: Rabbi, the Jews but now sought to stone thee. And goest thou thither again?

9. Jesus answered: Are there not twelve hours of the day? If a man walk in the day, he stumbleth not, because he seeth the light of this world:

10. But if he walk in the night, he stumbleth, because the light is not in him.

11. These things he said; and after that he said to them: Lazarus our friend sleepeth; but I go that I may awake him out of sleep.

12. His disciples therefore said: Lord, if he sleep, he shall do well.

13. But Jesus spoke of his death; and they thought that he spoke of the repose of sleep.

14. Then therefore Jesus said to them plainly: Lazarus is dead.

15. And I am glad, for your sakes, that I was not there, that you may believe. But, let us go to him.

---

6. '*Therefore*' He remained where He was, i.e. till Lazarus should in fact be dead.

9. 'Twelve hours'; sunrise to sunset. That is, one must work to the very end, and can do so safely so long as light lasts. The simple statement seems however to suggest a further outlook, since 'the light of this *world*' inevitably recalls that that is what our Lord is (8: 12; 9: 5), and he has the light *in him* (cf. St John of the Cross: 'Without other light or lamp—Save that which in my heart was burning'; though see Luke 11: 34; Matt. 6: 23). If verse 8 suggests that the disciples thought our Lord

11. meant to be alone, 'Lazarus *our* friend' (verse 11) is almost a reproach: would they hesitate to come too?

12. Though 'to sleep' was easily used as meaning 'to be dead' (Matt. 27: 52; Acts 7: 60; 1 Cor. 15: 6, etc.), we can hardly be surprised if the disciples did *not* take it in that sense or foresee another 'resuscitation'.

15. The raising of Lazarus should have strengthened their faith in view of our Lord's own death *and* resurrection.

16. Thomas therefore, who is called Didymus, said to his fellow disciples: Let us also go, that we may die with him.

The Raising of Lazarus (ii): 17-31

17. Jesus therefore came: and found that he had been four days already in the grave.

18. (Now Bethania was near Jerusalem, about fifteen furlongs off.)

19. And many of the Jews were come to Martha and Mary, to comfort them concerning their brother.

20. Martha therefore, as soon as she heard that Jesus was come, went to meet him: but Mary sat at home.

21. Martha therefore said to Jesus: Lord, if thou hadst been here, my brother had not died.

22. But now also I know that whatsoever thou wilt ask of God, God will give it thee.

23. Jesus saith to her: Thy brother shall rise again.

24. Martha saith to him: I know that he shall rise again, in the resurrection at the last day.

25. Jesus said to her: I am the resurrection and the life: he that believeth in me, although he be dead, shall live:

---

16. The same love that prompted Thomas's readiness to die with Jesus made it impossible, later, for him to believe, at first, so joyous a news as the resurrection.

21. A sigh of regret that He had not been there: but it would probably have taken the messenger one day to reach our Lord; He remained two days at Bethany and took a day to return: Lazarus must therefore have died very soon after our Lord first heard of his illness.

22. A vague imperfect faith. Martha partly feels that our Lord would have prevented the death had He not been away, had He heard of it in time: but even as it is, if He asks for—for what? . . . She dares not put her hope into words.

23, 24. Lazarus *would* rise—but (24) Martha takes that as meaning at the Last Day and desponds. *That* would not satisfy her!

26. And every one that liveth and believeth in me shall not die for ever. Believest thou this?

27. She saith to him: Yea, Lord, I have believed that thou art Christ, the Son of the living God, who art come into this world.

28. And when she had said these things, she went and called her sister Mary secretly, saying: The master is come and calleth for thee.

29. She, as soon as she heard *this*, riseth quickly and cometh to him.

30. For Jesus was not yet come into the town: but he was still in that place where Martha had met him.

31. The Jews therefore, who were with her in the house and comforted her, when they saw Mary, that she rose up speedily and went out, followed her, saying: She goeth to the grave to weep there.

The Raising of Lazarus (iii): 32–44

32. When Mary therefore was come where Jesus was, seeing him, she fell down at his feet and saith to him: Lord, if thou hadst been here, my brother had not died.

33. Jesus, therefore, when he saw her weeping, and the Jews that were come with her weeping, groaned in the spirit and troubled himself.

25, 26. Jesus says: '*I am* the Resurrection and the Life': the former depends on the latter: 'He who believes in Me, *even if* he die (physically) shall live (both by resuscitation, and by means of "eternal life"); and all who are alive and believe in Me shall not die—for ever (though they die physically, that is not death "for ever")'. And He asks: 'Believest thou this?' And she makes her full Act of Faith—feeling no need to inquire further about Lazarus.

28–31. Our Lord has not *said* that He was calling Mary; but this is not an exhaustive verbatim record of the conversation. Martha tried to extricate her quietly from the crowd of mourners: useless: they insisted on coming with her.

32. Mary says what Martha did, but her cries of grief are twice insisted on.

33. 'Groaned'. The word ἐμβριμήσασθαι normally, and in

34. And said: Where have you laid him? They say to him: Lord, come and see.
35. And Jesus wept.
36. The Jews therefore said: Behold how he loved him.
37. But some of them said: Could not he that opened the eyes of the man born blind have caused that this man should not die?
38. Jesus therefore again groaning in himself, cometh to the sepulchre. Now it was a cave; and a stone was laid over it.
39. Jesus saith: Take away the stone. Martha, the sister of him that was dead, saith to him: Lord, by this time he stinketh, for he is now of four days.
40. Jesus saith to her: Did not I say to thee that if thou believe, thou shalt see the glory of God?
41. They took therefore the stone away. And Jesus lifting up his eyes, said: Father, I give thee thanks that thou hast heard me.

---

the N.T. (Matt. 9: 30; Mark 1: 43; 14: 5) is used of showing *indignation*. Against what was He indignant? We think, He felt an indignant sorrow, and shuddered, at the thought that this miracle, worked out of love, would be responsible for new hatred and even the resolve to kill Him (see verse 46). Still, ἐνεβριμήσατο used without an object need not mean anger, but any strong emotion or conflict of emotions.

35. Our Lord's tears may have been due to sympathy with the genuine sorrow around Him, and also, to sadness that hearts would actually be hardened by what He was going to do.
37. A few (τινές) notice Him weeping, and ask whether, if He loved Lazarus so much, He could not have prevented him from dying—after all, He had given sight to the blind man!
38. The tomb could be an excavation like a room having a round stone rolled before the entry (such seemingly was our Lord's tomb), or, a grave like ours with a stone put on the top: such probably was Lazarus's grave, though the text is not conclusive.
39. Martha who had half asked for a miracle, shrank back when the preliminaries were suggested.

42. And I knew that thou hearest me always; but because of the people who stand about have I said it, that they may believe that thou hast sent me.

43. When he had said these things, he cried with a loud voice: Lazarus, come forth.

44. And presently he that had been dead came forth, bound feet and hands with winding bands. And his face was bound about with a napkin. Jesus said to them: Loose him and let him go.

The Chief Priests and the Pharisees take counsel together: 45–56

45. Many therefore of the Jews, who were come to Mary and Martha and had seen the things that Jesus did, believed in him.

46. But some of them went to the Pharisees and told them the things that Jesus had done.

47. The chief priests, therefore, and the Pharisees gathered a council and said: What do we, for this man doth many miracles?

---

41. Our Lord truly prayed, and, as Man, had the duty of doing so: yet the knowledge of the harmony between His Will and His Father's enables Him to thank Him for granting His prayer even before it had been put into words: nor are words necessary for prayer. But He utters His thanks that the people may know that He *has* prayed and that the result may show that God approves Him and that from God He holds His mission.

44. Seemingly Lazarus stood up and came forth divinely supported, for St John insists that his feet were tied (so that he could not walk) and his hands (so that he could not untie the knots of the bandages), and that his face was covered (so that he could not see).

45, 46. Strange effect of the miracle! Many believed (in our Lord), but some, though they saw the marvel, went off to denounce Jesus—to the Pharisees, as being well-known for their hostility to Him; but when active measures are to be taken, the chief priests too must be convened.

47. 'What are we doing?' A rhetorical question—'Nothing!'

48. If we let him alone so, all will believe in him; and the Romans will come, and take away our place and nation.

49. But one of them, named Caiaphas, being the high priest that year, said to them: You know nothing.

50. Neither do you consider that it is expedient for you that one man should die for the people and that the whole nation perish not.

51. And this he spoke not of himself: but being the high priest of that year, he prophesied that Jesus should die for the nation.

52. And not only for the nation, but to gather together in one the children of God that were dispersed.

53. From that day therefore they devised to put him to death.

54. Wherefore Jesus walked no more openly among the Jews: but he went into a country near the desert, unto a city that is called Ephrem. And there he abode with his disciples.

55. And the pasch of the Jews was at hand: and many from the country went up to Jerusalem, before the pasch, to purify themselves.

56. They sought therefore for Jesus; and they discoursed one with another, standing in the temple: What think you that he is not come to the festival day? And the chief priests and Pharisees had given a commandment that, if any man knew where he was, he should tell, that they might apprehend him.

---

48. If the people acclaim him as Messias, Rome will make an end of the Temple (2 Macc. 5: 19) and the very nation.

49. Caiaphas was high-priest A.D. 18–36; 'that year', then, simply means 'the year in question', i.e. that of the Crucifixion.

50. That is, *whatever* Jesus is or claims or is thought to be, He is a national danger and must be eliminated.

51. God chooses His official representative to say what has a spiritual meaning of which he is unconscious: the 'one man', victim for the people, was to be He whose death would 'bring together into unity' all the 'children of God' scattered through the world and all the future.

54. Ephrem was some 20 miles N.E. of Jerusalem in a lonely region.

55. This Pasch is the third in John; cf. 2: 13; 6: 4.

CHAPTER TWELVE

Mary anoints Jesus: 1–11
(Mark 14: 3–9; Matt. 26: 6–13)

1. Jesus therefore, six days before the pasch, came to Bethania, where Lazarus had been dead, whom Jesus raised to life.
2. And they made him a supper there: and Martha served. But Lazarus was one of them that were at table with him.
3. Mary therefore took a pound of ointment of right spikenard, of great price, and anointed the feet of Jesus and wiped his feet with her hair. And the house was filled with the odour of the ointment.
4. Then one of his disciples, Judas Iscariot, he that was about to betray him, said:

---

1. The date is that of the supper, rather than of our Lord's arrival. It is the eighth day of Nisan, 'Saturday before Palm Sunday'.
2. The meal is at Simon the Leper's; Lazarus is a guest; Martha has been asked to help serve.
3. St Matthew and St Mark do not name Mary: it seems likely that the earlier tradition wished to keep the family—the two sisters and Lazarus—in the background lest their connection with our Lord should imperil them (cf. verse 10). 'Right' (πιστική), i.e. genuine. The ointment was *nardus spicatus*; St Matthew and St Mark speak only of the (normal) anointing of the head, though Mark 14: 8 ('anointed my body') suggests more than that. The whole act suggests the ardent devotion of Mary: without waiting for some napkin she uncovers her hair and uses it to wipe His feet. St John, alluding to the house being filled with the perfume, can hardly but refer to the Synoptists' comment that her action would be

5. Why was not this ointment sold for three hundred pence and given to the poor?

6. Now he said this, not because he cared for the poor; but because he was a thief and, having the purse, carried the things that were put therein.

7. Jesus therefore said: Let her alone, that she may keep it against the day of my burial.

8. For the poor you have always with you: but me you have not always.

9. A great multitude therefore of the Jews knew that he was there; and they came, not for Jesus' sake only, but that they might see Lazarus, whom he had raised from the dead.

10. But the chief priests thought to kill Lazarus also:

11. Because many of the Jews, by reason of him, went away and believed in Jesus.

---

preached throughout the world; but in itself it need have no symbolical meaning, and in Plutarch's Life of Alexander almost identical words are used of a house in which perfumes and myrrh had been poured out.

5. Judas was not presumably calculating the exact cost of the perfume; a *denarius* was a working-man's daily wage (cf. 6: 7): 300 denarii were, then, what a man would take nearly a year to earn.

6. 'Carried' ($\dot{\epsilon}\beta\acute{a}\sigma\tau\alpha\sigma\epsilon\nu$) could mean 'used to take from', i.e. stole. 'Purse'; more likely a 'money-box' ($\gamma\lambda\omega\sigma\sigma\acute{o}\kappa\omicron\mu\omicron\nu$). There was then a box for alms, but it is not clear that Judas was the regular 'treasurer'.

7. The construction implies an ellipse: 'Let her alone: (she did not use it before) in order that she might keep it in view of the day of My burial': cf. 1: 8; 6: 30, 50; 9: 3.

11. 'Went away', i.e. left the party of the priests and joined our Lord.

John abbreviates, adding only that part of the crowd was composed of those who had witnessed or heard of the raising of Lazarus.

Jesus enters Jerusalem: 12–19
(Matt. 21: 1–11; Mark 11: 1–11; and Luke 19: 29–45)

12. And on the next day, a great multitude that was come to the festival day, when they had heard that Jesus was coming to Jerusalem,

13. Took branches of palm trees and went forth to meet him and cried: Hosanna. Blessed is he that cometh in the name of the Lord, the king of Israel.

14. And Jesus found a young ass and sat upon it, as it is written:

15. *Fear not, daughter of Sion: behold, thy king cometh, sitting on an ass's colt.*

16. These things his disciples did not know at the first: but when Jesus was glorified, then they remembered that these things were written of him and that they had done these things to him.

17. The multitude therefore gave testimony, which was with him, when he called Lazarus out of the grave and raised him from the dead.

18. For which reason also the people came to meet him, because they heard that he had done this miracle.

19. The Pharisees therefore said among themselves: Do you see that we prevail nothing? Behold, the whole world is gone after him.

---

13. 'Hosanna' means 'Save, we pray': it now was no more than a shout of welcome. Translate: 'Blessed *be* He . . .'; and read: '*and* the King of Israel', i.e., 'He, He, the King of Israel', not merely 'the king of the Jews' (18: 33, 37, etc.), but the descendant of David and heir of the promises made to him.

15. St John too quotes Zach. 9: 9, but loosely: 'Fear not!' (instead of 'exult') somewhat underlines the pacific nature of this arrival.

16. The relation of prophetic words to historic reality was understood only after the resurrection (cf. 2: 22; 7: 39; 20: 9).

19. A picturesque exaggeration, though St John writing maybe 70 years later, could indeed see that men from all over the world were coming to Jesus (cf. verse 32).

Gentiles desire to see our Lord: 20–26

20. Now there were certain Gentiles among them, who came up to adore on the festival day.

21. These therefore came to Philip, who was of Bethsaida of Galilee, and desired him, saying: Sir, we would see Jesus.

22. Philip cometh and telleth Andrew. Again Andrew and Philip told Jesus.

23. But Jesus answered them, saying: The hour is come that the Son of man should be glorified.

24. Amen, amen, I say to you, unless the grain of wheat falling into the ground die,

25. Itself remaineth alone. But if it die, it bringeth forth much fruit. He that loveth his life shall lose it: and he that hateth his life in this world keepeth it unto life eternal.

26. If any man minister to me, let him follow me; and where I am, there also shall my minister be. If any man minister to me, him will my Father honour.

---

20. These 'Greeks' probably were ex-pagans, attracted by Jewish monotheism, and liking to visit Jerusalem, e.g. at the Pasch. They may have been moved simply by curiosity (characteristic of the Greeks), and have approached Philip because of

21. his Greek name, especially as Bethsaida, though by the Lake of Galilee, was east of the Jordan and therefore in the domain of the tetrarch Philip. Anyhow they disappear: St John constantly allows his 'stories' to melt into a doctrinal discourse of our Lord's. Philip consults Andrew, his compatriot, whose name too was Greek, and they tell our Lord.

23. In St John, our Lord's 'glorification' is His saving death. The grain, disappearing and reappearing in a full field of wheat, recalls Mark 4: 26 ff. rather than the parable of the Sower.

25. This is the emphatic doctrine in the Synoptists; cf. Mark 8: 31–35; Matt. 10: 29; 16: 21–25; Luke 9: 22–24; 17: 33. In all

Jesus foretells His death: 27–36a

27. Now is my soul troubled. And what shall I say? Father, save me from this hour. But for this cause I came unto this hour.
28. Father, glorify thy name. A voice therefore came from heaven: I have both glorified it and will glorify it again.
29. The multitude therefore that stood and heard said that it thundered. Others said: An angel spoke to him.
30. Jesus answered and said: This voice came not because of me, but for your sakes.
31. Now is the judgment of the world: now shall the prince of this world be cast out.

---

cases, the idea of following our Lord and here of ministering to Him, is connected with abdication of this-world ambitions—*God* will honour His Son's disciple.

27. Our Lord is in a state of anguish (τετάρακται : perfect) because of His sense that death is now so near. What is He to say? 'Father, save me from this hour?' No! It was through His saving death that God was to be glorified, so what *could* He say other than: 'Glorify Thy name!' This is a foretaste of the Agony in the Garden, that St John does not relate.
28. 'It' refers to the Name of God, that is, God Himself, who has already won glory through the life and miracles of his Son, and will continue to do so by His resurrection and what followed it.
29. Possibly each heard what he was 'attuned' to: possibly too all felt there had been *some* heavenly response: thunder was called in the O.T. the voice of God: messages by means of angels were frequently read of there: and cf. Acts, 23: 9.
31. Our Lord regards His 'hour' as actually begun: the world, rejecting Christ, stands condemned: Satan, 'ruler' of that world, is about to be cast out (cf. 14: 30; 16: 11; Matt. 4: 8; Luke 4: 6). Christ's victory is assured, though we still have to fight (Col. 2: 15, etc.).

32. And I, if I be lifted up from the earth, will draw all things to myself.

33. (Now this he said, signifying what death he should die.)

34. The multitude answered him: We have heard out of the law that Christ abideth for ever. And how sayest thou: The Son of man must be lifted up? Who is this Son of man?

35. Jesus therefore said to them: Yet a little while, the light is among you. Walk whilst you have the light, that the darkness overtake you not. And he that walketh in darkness knoweth not whither he goeth.

36. Whilst you have the light, believe in the light, that you may be the children of light.

Some believe in Him secretly: 36b–43

These things Jesus spoke: and he went away and hid himself from them.

37. And whereas he had done so many miracles before them, they believed not in him:

38. That the saying of Isaias the prophet might be fulfilled, which he said: *Lord, who hath believed our hearing? And to whom hath the arm of the Lord been revealed?*[1]

32, 33. Lest 'to be lifted up' should be taken as 'to be exalted', i.e. in glory, St John explains (33) that our Lord 'indicated' the crucifixion: 'signifying' ($\sigma\eta\mu\alpha\acute{\iota}\nu\omega\nu$) is often thus used both of pagan oracles and of veiled prophecies (e.g. Dan. 21: 45; John 18: 32, etc.; Apoc. 1: 1).

34. By 'the Law' all the O.T. is meant, cf. 10: 34; 15: 25. It seemed clear that the reign of the Messias should have no end; but Jesus has indicated that in *some* way He is to depart. But (verse 23) He has presented Himself as Son of Man. Who, then, *is* this Son of Man? If not the Messias, then who?

35, 36. Again, our Lord will not define Himself: by now they ought to have understood that He was the 'Light' (3: 19, etc.), and that by faith in Him men would walk in the light and not be overtaken by the darkness. This is the last public discourse that John selects for recording.

[1] Isaias 53: 1

39. Therefore they could not believe, because Isaias said again:

40. *He hath blinded their eyes and hardened their heart, that they should not see with their eyes, nor understand with their heart and be converted: and I should heal them.*

41. These things said Isaias, when he saw his glory and spoke of him.

42. However, many of the chief men also believed in him; but because of the Pharisees they did not confess *him*, that they might not be cast out of the synagogue.

43. For they loved the glory of men more than the glory of God.

'A Light into the World': 44–50

44. But Jesus cried and said: He that believeth in me doth not believe in me, but in him that sent me.

45. And he that seeth me, seeth him that sent me.

---

38. 'Our hearing': either, 'what we have heard from Thee', or, more probably, 'what they have heard from us': see Is. 52: 15; 53: 1. Cf. Rom. 10: 16. The second quotation is from Is. 6: 9, 10, used in Matt. 13: 14, 15; Acts 28: 25–27, and Rom. 11: 8. The point is, that if grace be constantly resisted, men become *unable* to accept God's revelation, short of a new overwhelming grace. In verse 41 St John suggests that when Isaias saw the glory of God (6: 1–5) it was that too of Jesus. Jesus *was* God's glory, revealed to men. Verses 44–50 are a brief résumé of our Lord's teaching, or quite possibly some lines have been misplaced in the original version, and verses 36–43 should follow verses 44–50. In any case, we know from the Synoptists that our Lord spoke much in public during the last week of His life.

44. It is clear from verse 36 our Lord has gone away and 'hidden' Himself, and St John relates the tragic unsuccess of our Lord's words or even miracles. Then we abruptly have these verses saying that Jesus 'cried aloud and said . . .'. Either, then, they should have preceded 36b, or, we think, they are St John's own

46. I am come, a light into the world, that whosoever believeth in me may not remain in darkness.

47. And if any man hear my words and keep them not, I do not judge him: for I came not to judge the world, but to save the world.

48. He that despiseth me and receiveth not my words hath one that judgeth him. The word that I have spoken, the same shall judge him in the last day.

49. For I have not spoken of myself: but the Father who sent me, he gave me commandment what I should say and what I should speak.

50. And I know that his commandment is life everlasting. The things therefore that I speak, even as the Father said unto me, so do I speak.

---

résumé of our Lord's teaching. No hint is given of where Jesus spoke them or when. 'Does not believe in Me but in . . .' A good example of the Hebrews' way of saying 'does not' (etc.), meaning 'not *merely*'. He who was *sent*, so that belief in Him demanded belief in God who sent Him. Yet, there is a mysterious unity between *this* 'Sent' and the Sender (verse 45: and 14: 7, 9).

46. Either: 'I, Light, am come . . .', or, 'I am come as a Light.' . . .

47, 48. Cf. 3: 17: 'judge' ($\kappa\rho\acute{\iota}\sigma\iota\varsigma$) means 'condemnation', or a 'division', or hovers between the two. The object of His coming was not condemnation but salvation: none the less, some would believe His words; some, not. Those who culpably refuse to do so, are set apart for condemnation. The voice of Jesus is the voice of God. Thus ends the first part of the Gospel according to St John.

CHAPTER THIRTEEN

The Last Supper; The Washing of the Feet: 1–11

1. Before the festival day of the pasch, Jesus knowing that his hour was come, that he should pass out of this world to the Father: having loved his own who were in the world, he loved them unto the end.

2. And when supper was done (the devil having now put into the heart of Judas Iscariot, the son of Simon, to betray him),

3. Knowing that the Father had given him all things into his hands and that he came from God and goeth to God;

4. He riseth from supper and layeth aside his garments and, having taken a towel, girded himself.

5. After that, he putteth water into a basin and began to wash the feet of the disciples and to wipe them with the towel wherewith he was girded.

6. He cometh therefore to Simon Peter. And Peter saith to him: Lord, dost thou wash my feet?

---

1. Thursday evening, presumably before 6 P.M. when the Pasch (including its 'preparation') could be considered to have begun. 'To the end'; i.e. not only till His actual death but 'to the utmost'.

2. 'Was done': rather 'was taking place' ($\gamma\epsilon\nu o\mu\acute{\epsilon}\nu o\upsilon$): it is not implied that the supper was finished; but, that it had been prepared, or (especially if we read $\gamma\iota\gamma\nu o\mu\acute{\epsilon}\nu o\upsilon$, the present tense) that it was divided into two parts, the washing of the feet coming between them.

3. These solemn words emphasize the humility of our Lord's act.

4. 'Garments' ($\iota\mu\acute{\alpha}\tau\iota\alpha$): the plural is unusual; perhaps the cloak and girdle.

6. He may have come first to Peter, for it is unlikely that he

7. Jesus answered and said to him: What I do, thou knowest not now; but thou shalt know hereafter.

8. Peter saith to him: Thou shalt never wash my feet. Jesus answered him: If I wash thee not, thou shalt have no part with me.

9. Simon Peter saith to him: Lord, not only my feet, but also my hands and my head.

10. Jesus saith to him: He that is washed needeth not but to wash his feet, but is clean wholly. And you are clean, but not all.

11. For he knew who he was that would betray him; therefore he said: You are not all clean.

Jesus the Example: 12–20

12. Then after he had washed their feet and taken his garments, being set down again, he said to them: Know you what I have done to you?

13. You call me Master and Lord. And you say well: for so I am.

14. If then I being *your* Lord and Master, have washed your feet; you also ought to wash one another's feet.

15. For I have given you an example, that as I have done to you, so you do also.

---

should have allowed others to be washed before making his protest. The Greek (σύ μου) marks an emphasis—'*You* wash *my* feet?'

8. The best parallel is the Baptist's shrinking from baptizing Jesus (Matt. 3: 14).

10. 'He who is bathed' (λελουμένος): those who seek a mystical sense in this incident, say that the Apostles had received sanctifying grace, and needed only to have the daily venial faults washed away. Jesus may well have had some deep symbolical meaning in His mind; but He does not expect the Apostles to understand even the moral meaning of this act.

14. 'I, *the* Lord and *the* Teacher': makes a strong emphasis.

15. Here the 'example' is clearly seen to have a moral value: the

16. Amen, amen, I say to you: The servant is not greater than his lord: neither is the apostle greater than he that sent him.

17. If you know these things, you shall be blessed if you do them.

18. I speak not of you all: I know whom I have chosen. But that the scripture may be fulfilled: *He that eateth bread with me shall lift up his heel against me.*

19. At present I tell you, before it come to pass: that when it shall come to pass, you may believe that I am he.

20. Amen, amen, I say to you, he that receiveth whomsoever I send receiveth me: and he that receiveth me receiveth him that sent me.

Apostles will not have thought that our Lord's example was confined to literal washing of men's feet.

18. From Ps. 41 (40: Vg.), 10: the picture is that of a horse kicking backwards.

19. 'At present'; i.e. an emphatic '*now*', like 14: 29. The Apostles could not imagine that one of themselves would betray Him: but when it had happened, they would remember He had foretold it, and realize still better that He 'was', i.e. all that He had assured them of: here it is hardly the divine Name 'I am': possibly 'he of whom the prophet spoke', but probably the words are more inclusive than that.

20. How do these words follow what precedes? (See Matt. 10: 40.) 'Amen, amen' often introduces some idea that gives a new development to what precedes. Perhaps our Lord was foreseeing the career of His apostles but was interrupted by the thought of the imminent betrayal—no one *would* receive Judas (see next verse). Cf. 12: 27, where the close approach of death overwhelms Him. We do not think Judas was present at the institution of the Eucharist. We think that there were two parts to the meal: after an 'introduction', the anticipated paschal feast: then, in parenthesis, the washing of the feet and the denunciation of the traitor and his departure: then the second part (for which they thought He had gone out to buy something); then the Eucharist and Discourses.

The Traitor: 21–30

(cf. Matt. 26: 21–25; Mark 14: 18–21; Luke 22: 21–23)

21. When Jesus had said these things, he was troubled in spirit; and he testified, and said: Amen, amen, I say to you, one of you shall betray me.

22. The disciples therefore looked one upon another, doubting of whom he spoke.

23. Now there was leaning on Jesus' bosom one of his disciples, whom Jesus loved.

24. Simon Peter therefore beckoned to him and said to him: Who is it of whom he speaketh?

25. He therefore, leaning on the breast of Jesus, saith to him: Lord, who is it?

26. Jesus answered: He it is to whom I shall reach bread dipped. And when he had dipped the bread, he gave it to Judas Iscariot, *the son* of Simon.

27. And after the morsel, Satan entered into him. And Jesus said to him: That which thou dost, do quickly.

---

21. 'Testified': He speaks openly—almost as a witness might testify to the guilt of an accused man.

22. In Matt. and Mark each actually asks if the traitor could be he: in Luke they speak to one another—in John, the inquiry is but by a look.

23–25. Presumably those present were lying on long cushions, in an arc of a circle, their left elbow on a low table, their right hand free to take the food. Thus if St John was on our Lord's right, his head would have been roughly at the level of His breast; he had, then, only to lean his head back a little in order to whisper to him. It is simplest to suppose that St Peter was similarly on St John's right, and able to whisper to him, and ask him to ask our Lord, which he did.

26. This 'morsel' (of bread or perhaps meat) dipped into the dish of sauce cannot have been the Eucharist: but it was none the less disloyal to accept this mark of friendship when Judas's

28. Now no man at the table knew to what purpose he said this unto him.

29. For some thought, because Judas had the purse, that Jesus had said to him: Buy those things which we have need of for the festival day: or that he should give something to the poor.

30. He therefore, having received the morsel, went out immediately. And it was night.

The New Commandment: 31–38

31. When he therefore was gone out, Jesus said: Now is the Son of man glorified; and God is glorified in him.

32. If God be glorified in him, God also will glorify him in himself: and immediately will he glorify him.

---

27. mind was already made up, and Satan could the more easily control his will. Our Lord, unable to do more for him, and feeling the weight of his presence intolerable, told him to go, and be finished with his evil work.

29. 'For the feast': difficult to explain. Perhaps the reference is to other special meals eaten during the paschal octave: the Apostles could not think that the paschal meal could be eaten on two successive days; nor that a further meal could have been eaten after the paschal one.

30. We cannot reasonably join the words: 'It was night' with the following words, nor take it merely as a statement of the time at which Judas left. It was 'night' in the traitor's heart; and, humanly speaking, the Light of the world was about to be quenched: yet in the very next words our Lord shows how differently He thinks of His Passion.

31, 32. Our Lord's miracles had, from the first, glorified Him (2: 11); but His death and triumph over death were to be His supreme glorification, and all the glory that was and should be His, redounds to the glory of His Father. The rest of the verse probably means that as our Lord has glorified God during His human life, and has been and will be glorified by His Father during it, so God will glorify His Son in eternity—

33. Little children, yet a little while I am with you. You shall seek me. And as I said to the Jews: Whither I go you cannot come; so I say to you now.

34. A new commandment I give unto you: That you love one another, as I have loved you, that you also love one another.

35. By this shall all men know that you are my disciples, if you have love one for another.

36. Simon Peter saith to him: Lord, whither goest thou? Jesus answered: Whither I go, thou canst not follow me now: but thou shalt follow hereafter.

37. Peter saith to him: Why cannot I follow thee now? I will lay down my life for thee.

38. Jesus answered him: Wilt thou lay down thy life for me? Amen, amen, I say to thee, the cock shall not crow, till thou deny me thrice.

---

the Humanity shall no more be in any sense a veil for the Divinity.

33. Our Lord begins a saddening statement with the tender word 'Little children': what had been said to the Jews (7: 34; 8: 21) has to be said also to the disciples, yet in how different a tone! How was the commandment 'new'? The O.T. itself had enjoined the love of one's neighbour (cf. on Luke 10: 27); and our Lord had made that command (including love for enemies) no less cogent than that for God: but never yet had He offered His own love for His disciples as the measure of that which they should have for one another.

35. The first result of this love should be that 'others' would cry out at the sight of the love existing *among* Christians: but it was not to be an exclusive love like that of the Jewish 'community': if Christ's love was to be the model, no one at all could be excluded from its embrace.

36. Peter has not understood verse 33 as implying death. He is distressed by the idea that Jesus is going anywhere whither he cannot go too. Our Lord softens His words by telling Peter that in time he shall follow Him—even by death for His sake that Peter so fervently says he is ready to suffer. For this prediction of the denial, see Matt. 26: 31–35; Mark 14: 27–31; Luke 22: 31–34. St Mark and St Matthew place the prediction on the way to Gethsemani and do not speak of the flight of the Apostles. Only St Mark speaks of a second cock-crow. The substance of the prediction and events is the same in all: the Evangelists often record them in orders that differ chronologically.

CHAPTER FOURTEEN

The Last Discourse (i): 1–14

1. Let not your heart be troubled. You believe in God: believe also in me.

2. In my Father's house there are many mansions. If not, I would have told you: because I go to prepare a place for you.

3. And if I shall go and prepare a place for you, I will come again and will take you to myself: that where I am, you also may be.

---

1. The Apostles were troubled especially by the idea of separation so firmly foretold. 'Believe' (πιστεύετε) might be, both times, an imperative: but the point is, throughout, that they must believe in Him as they do in God; the meaning is *both* 'intellectual' belief, and trust.

2. The first part of the verse is clear: there is plenty of room in God's house for all of them. The more obvious meaning of what follows is: 'If it were not so, I would have told you that I am going (i.e. on my way) thither to prepare a place for you.'

3. Verse 3 then follows: 'And when I shall have gone, and shall have prepared you a place, I will come back and fetch you.' The difficulty is that our Lord does not have to go to ensure lodgings, so to say, for the Apostles: such places are there from eternity. Others, then, admit a sort of parable: 'The *places* are there, no doubt: but I am going ahead to make them *ready* for you.' If this seems too 'materialist', we can translate: 'There is plenty of room for all of you in heaven: if there were not, I would have told you that I am going to *make* room for you. And even if I do go away and make room for you, I will come again, etc.' This 'taking them to Himself' does not

116

4. And whither I go you know: and the way you know.
5. Thomas saith to him: Lord, we know not whither thou goest. And how can we know the way?
6. Jesus saith to him: I am the way, and the truth, and the life. No man cometh to the Father, but by me.
7. If you had known me, you would without doubt have known my Father also: and from henceforth you shall know him. And you have seen him.
8. Philip saith to him: Lord, shew us the Father; and it is enough for us.
9. Jesus saith to him: Have I been so long a time with you and have you not known me? Philip, he that seeth me seeth the Father also. How sayest thou: Shew us the Father?
10. Do you not believe that I am in the Father and the Father in me? The words that I speak to you, I speak not of myself. But the Father who abideth in me, he doth the works.
11. Believe you not that I am in the Father and the Father in me?

---

allude to any fixed time: He would come at the proper hour for each to be taken from this world.
4. More generally: 'And whither I go, you know the way to it.'
5. The immediate future, at any rate, is obscure. Thomas asks what they are to do *now*.
6. This sums up the whole of our Lord's self-revelation.
7. Read: 'If you have known Me (as you have!), you will know also the Father: (and) already you know Him and are seeing Him ($\dot{\epsilon}\omega\rho\acute{\alpha}\kappa\alpha\tau\epsilon$; perfect).'
8. Philip cannot realize that to see Jesus is to see God Himself: perhaps he wishes for a vision such as that of Moses (Ex. 33: 18 ff. or Is. 6: 1).
9, 10. He who has *understood* ($\ddot{\epsilon}\gamma\nu\omega\kappa\alpha\varsigma$) Jesus has *seen* the Father, though by faith alone. What Jesus says, is said by the Father: and the Father, dwelling in Jesus, does His works (read $\pi o\iota\epsilon\hat{\iota}\ \tau\grave{\alpha}\ \ddot{\epsilon}\rho\gamma\alpha\ \alpha\dot{\upsilon}\tau o\hat{\upsilon}$).
11. By sheer contact with Him, they ought to be able to believe that the Father is in Him: failing that, let them believe because of the works they have seen Him do!

12. Otherwise believe for the very works' sake. Amen, amen, I say to you, he that believeth in me, the works that I do, he also shall do: and greater than these shall he do.

13. Because I go to the Father: and whatsoever you shall ask the Father in my name, that will I do: that the Father may be glorified in the Son.

14. If you shall ask me any thing in my name, that I will do.

The Last Discourse (ii): *The Paraclete:* 15-24

15. If you love me, keep my commandments.

16. And I will ask the Father: and he shall give you another Paraclete, that he may abide with you for ever:

12-14. Our Lord then promises that they shall do even greater works than these, and that whatever they ask 'in His name', *He* will do it. The works will be 'greater', because our Lord's visible mission was only to the Jews: but above all, the unseen ministry of grace which should be exercised throughout the world would be essentially greater than even the raising of a dead man like Lazarus. 'In My name' may mean that we pray to God 'through' Jesus Christ, as the Liturgy does; or in His very person. When we ask what can *not* be asked thus, clearly He will not grant it: at Mass the Church says: 'through Him, and along with Him, and *in* Him' all glory comes to God.

16. The sense of Paraclete (Παράκλητος), *Advocatus*, is difficult to define; so the Vulgate does not try to translate it. It first meant, as a rule, someone you called to your side if you were on trial, in no legal position but to 'back you up' in presence of the judges and prosecutor—an aged mother or destitute children could fill the role. Later it meant more nearly 'counsel for the defence', or one who encourages and comforts, or gives advice. 'Spirit', to us, means (when not directly contrasted with the body, or mankind living on earth) something 'innermost' and invisible, and a 'driving force'. A shabby club may possess an excellent 'spirit': a man may be 'spirited' or 'spiritless'. Our Lord is already a

118

17. The spirit of truth, whom the world cannot receive, because it seeth him not, nor knoweth him. But you shall know him; because he shall abide with you and shall be in you.

18. I will not leave you orphans: I will come to you.

19. Yet a little while and the world seeth me no more. But you see me: because I live, and you shall live.

20. In that day you shall know that I am in my Father: and you in me, and I in you.

21. He that hath my commandments and keepeth them; he it is that loveth me. And he that loveth me shall be loved of my Father: and I will love him and will manifest myself to him.

22. Judas saith to him, not the Iscariot: Lord, how is it that thou wilt manifest thyself to us, and not to the world?

23. Jesus answered and said to him: If any one love me, he will keep my word. And my Father will love him: and we will come to him and will make our abode with him.

'paraclete' (1 John 2: 1): He will ask for, and obtain, *another* one who will remain with His disciples *for ever* (therefore, with the Church), as His visible presence has not done; the world *cannot* see the invisible.

17–21. But those who 'keep' ($\tau\eta\rho\epsilon\hat{\iota}\nu$) His commandments (as *His*, not e.g. for convention's sake) show that they love Him, and will be loved all the more both by the Father and the Son who will make Himself still more 'realized' by them. This 'manifestation' will not be made by physical apparitions, or even by the infusion of new clear ideas: but the faithful soul will have an interior knowledge of God's presence save when God may choose to lead it still higher by means of complete 'desolation': but that is not being considered here.

22. Jude cannot understand a manifestation that will not be made to, and convince, the world. 'Jude'; only here in John, and not in Matthew or Mark, though in Luke 6: 16. Perhaps he came to be called 'Thaddeus' (so, Matt. 10: 3; Mark 3: 18) purposely to avoid the confusion which John explicitly prevents here. Our Lord does not answer him precisely, but

24. He that loveth me not keepeth not my words. And the word which you have heard is not mine; but the Father's who sent me.

Our Lord leaves Peace as His Bequest: 25-31

25. These things have I spoken to you, abiding with you.

26. But the Paraclete, the Holy Ghost, whom the Father will send in my name, he will teach you all things and bring all things to your mind, whatsoever I shall have said to you.

27. Peace I leave with you: my peace I give unto you: not as the world giveth, do I give unto you. Let not your heart be troubled: nor let it be afraid.

28. You have heard that I said to you: I go away, and I come unto you. If you loved me, you would indeed be glad, because I go to the Father: for the Father is greater than I.

---

reinforces what He has taught. But the indirect answer is, that the manifestation of which He speaks is to be made only to those who love and follow Him.

24. He has often said that His word is the Father's word (7: 16; 8: 26; 12: 49): similarly, His coming and abiding imply those too of the Father.

25. 'Abiding', i.e. during His earthly sojourn.

26. The 'office' of the Holy Spirit is both to recall what has been said, and to teach men to see deeper into that doctrine—not to teach new things. Between the Ascension and the death of the last Apostle, there may have been further revelations: even so, it will have been a deeper understanding of the implications of our Lord's doctrine and ordinances, e.g. about the Sacraments.

27. Our Lord reverts to the beginning of this discourse—they are *not* to be troubled, but interiorly at peace—not that the *world's* peace will be theirs! This is not the conventional Jewish 'goodbye'—'I give you peace!' Our Lord 'leaves' peace as His bequest: *His* peace, and not the 'peace' that can be given or even wished for by the world.

29. And now I have told you before it come to pass: that when it shall come to pass, you may believe.

30. I will not now speak many things with you. For the prince of this world cometh: and in me he hath not any thing.

31. But that the world may know that I love the Father: and as the Father hath given me commandment, so do I. Arise, let us go hence.

---

28. This does not mean (what is obvious) that man is less than God: nor yet that the Son of God, who is Himself God, is somehow less than God: but that as God Incarnate—which He has been and ever will be—He has lived a human life inferior to the glorified life which will soon be His.

29. Cf. 13: 19; 16: 4.

30. The Prince, or Chief of this world is Satan, and has no part in Jesus, and no power over Him. The world must recognize that He loves the Father, and that He is acting according to the Father's command, and by no means because the Devil, or his agents, force Him to act.

31. The last words certainly mean that our Lord gives the signal to leave the supper-room and the house in which it is.

This being admitted, where were chapters 15-17 spoken? Chapter 18 begins: 'Having thus spoken, Jesus went out with His disciples', which certainly suggests that He left the house where the Supper had taken place. It is impossible to suppose that He spoke and prayed the words of these chapters in the crowded streets (loud enough to be heard by all the Twelve) and arbitrary to say that they paused in the Temple. It is admitted by all that St Matthew placed together sentences spoken at different times, e.g. in the Sermon on the Mount, the instruction to the Apostles, and the Eschatological discourse (Chapters 5-7; 10: 6-42; 24): the order in which sentences are quoted is not affected by Inspiration. However, Chapters 14 and 18 here are manifestly wholes: but 15-17 contain repetitions of what was said in 14, yet also contain ideas that are new but in keeping with 14. We think, then, that St John, having written 14, may have reflected further, and written a sort of supplement, rather as Chapter 21 seems to have been. We are inclined to think that Chapters 15 and 16 were in fact added later, while the prayer in Chapter 17 was spoken just before the supper-room was left, but most suitably placed by St John at the end of all this section. The words: 'Arise, let us go hence' would have been overlooked, as might easily have happened if the gospel was written on loose sheets and arranged by one of St John's disciples.

CHAPTER FIFTEEN

The True Vine: 1–10

1. I am the true vine: and my Father is the husbandman.
2. Every branch in me that beareth not fruit, he will take away: and every one that beareth fruit, he will purge it, that it may bring forth more fruit.
3. Now you are clean, by reason of the word which I have spoken to you.
4. Abide in me: and I in you. As the branch cannot bear fruit of itself, unless it abide in the vine, so neither can you, unless you abide in me.
5. I am the vine: you the branches. He that abideth in me, and I in him, the same beareth much fruit: for without me you can do nothing.
6. If any one abide not in me, he shall be cast forth as a branch and shall wither: and they shall gather him up and cast him into the fire: and he burneth.

---

1. The Vine was very often used in O.T. as a name for Israel (Is. 5: 1; Jer. 2: 21; Ez. 15: 2; 17: 6, etc.): God is He who plants and tends the vine. Here, though the parable is all about the vine (Christ) and its branches, the latter are to be pruned or cut off altogether: but the vine cannot do that for itself, so the vine-tender must be introduced. The 'true' vine—either as contrasted with faithless Israel, or, as giving the only 'true', because supernatural, life.

2. Some branches are barren, and must be cut off altogether; others, though healthy, still need 'cleansing'; useless twigs are pruned away. But the parable must not be forced into an allegory.

3. 'Now you are *already* clean': our Lord's word has been efficacious (cf. 14: 10; Rom. 1: 16; 1 Peter 1: 23).

6. Our Lord does not mention the possibility of repentance. The

7. If you abide in me and my words abide in you, you shall ask whatever you will: and it shall be done unto you.

8. In this is my Father glorified: that you bring forth very much fruit and become my disciples.

9. As the Father hath loved me, I also have loved you. Abide in my love.

10. If you keep my commandments, you shall abide in my love: as I also have kept my Father's commandments and do abide in his love.

The New Commandment: 11–17

11. These things I have spoken to you, that my joy may be in you, and your joy may be filled.

12. This is my commandment, that you love one another, as I have loved you.

13. Greater love than this no man hath, that a man lay down his life for his friends.

14. You are my friends, if you do the things that I command you.

---

soul can, by mortal sin, cut itself off from the vine-stock: but there is always hope for it till death decides its fate.

7. Possibly this is said in view of what follows—the disciples are not to fear asking for *much*; for the Father's glory is, precisely, that they should bear *much* fruit and so become in the full sense His disciples; cf. verse 16.

11. As the Father is well-pleased with His Son, so Jesus has joy in His faithful, and *their* joy also must be full-filled, brim-ful: cf. the Baptist's joy, 3: 29: and 16: 24; 1 John 1: 4; Rom. 15: 13.

13. We note our Lord's 'modesty'; He does not insist that that is exactly what *He* is going to do: see 1 John 3: 11.

14. We remain Christ's servants, but ours is to be a loving service: perfect confidence exists between Christ and His beloved: 16: 12 does not contradict this—our Lord has told 'everything', the whole substance of His message: the Apostles may yet receive new revelations, and the Church will be ever guided into seeing more deeply into what they will teach.

15. I will not now call you servants: for the servant knoweth not wha his lord doth. But I have called you friends: because all things, whatsoever I have heard of my Father, I have made known to you.

16. You have not chosen me: but I have chosen you; and have appointed you, that you should go and should bring forth fruit; and your fruit should remain: that whatsoever you shall ask of the Father in my name, he may give it you.

17. These things I command you, that you love one another.

Master and Servant: Father and Son: 18–27

18. If the world hate you, know ye that it hath hated me before you.

19. If you had been of the world, the world would love its own: but because you are not of the world, but I have chosen you out of the world, therefore the world hateth you.

20. Remember my word that I said to you: The servant is not greater than his master. If they have persecuted me, they will also persecute you. If they have kept my word, they will keep yours also.

21. But all these things they will do to you for my name's sake: because they know not him that sent me.

22. If I had not come and spoken to them, they would not have sin: but now they have no excuse for their sin.

23. He that hateth me hateth my Father also.

---

16. The verbs are aorist: 'You did not choose Me: *I* chose you', and gave you your vocation. The parable of the vine is dropped, though it makes the use of the word 'fruit' more easy.

17. 'These things'—almost a paradox: 'I command you one thing—yet it contains all the rest.'

18. Cf. Matt. 24: 9; Mark 13: 13; Luke 21: 17; I John 3: 13.

20. Cf. 13: 16; but after verse 14 it seems surprising thus to revert to 'servant-hood'. Probably similar words were often spoken by Christ.

22. The 'sin' is to hate Him though He has come, spoken and worked His miracles.

24. If I had not done among them the works that no other man hath done, they would not have sin: but now they have both seen and hated both me and my Father.
25. But that the word may be fulfilled which is written in their law: *They hated me without cause.*
26. But when the Paraclete cometh, whom I will send you from the Father, the Spirit of truth, who proceedeth from the Father, he shall give testimony of me.
27. And you shall give testimony, because you are with me from the beginning.

---

25. From Ps. 24: 19 or 68: 5.
27. The Greek has the present: 'You *are* witnessing . . .'; that is, you are already fit to witness, and shall actually do so when the Spirit is given to you: cf. Matt. 10: 20; Mark 13: 11; Luke 12: 12.

CHAPTER SIXTEEN

Our Lord's Approaching Departure: 1–11

1. These things have I spoken to you, that you may not be scandalized.
2. They will put you out of the synagogues: yea, the hour cometh, that whosoever killeth you will think that he doth a service to God.
3. And these things will they do to you; because they have not known the Father nor me.
4. But these things I have told you, that when the hour shall come, you may remember that I told you of them.
5. But I told you not these things from the beginning, because I was with you. And now I go to him that sent me, and none of you asketh me: Whither goest thou?

---

1. ff. There should be no division between this chapter and Chapter 15. 'Scandalized', 'taken aback', perhaps to the point of losing trust in their Master.
2. For some time the Jews were more eager to denounce the Christians than were the pagans themselves. In the Synoptists (cf. Matt. 5: 11; 10: 17; 24: 9 and parallel passages in Mark and Luke) 'kings' are alluded to, persecution by the State being foretold as well as by the Jews.
4. Either our Lord means that He had not foretold the future so emphatically before, though the prophecies in the Synoptists were extremely emphatic: it is possible that St Matthew inserted into his Chapter 10 words used at the Last Supper: or else we think that possibly St John may have recorded this passage about persecutions separately, and have placed it here, as supplement to Chapter 14.
5. From here to the end of the chapter, our Lord speaks about His own departure, the Coming of the Spirit, and His own

6. But because I have spoken these things to you, sorrow hath filled your heart.

7. But I tell you the truth: it is expedient to you that I go. For if I go not, the Paraclete will not come to you: but if I go, I will send him to you.

8. And when he is come, he will convince the world of sin and of justice and of judgment.

9. Of sin: because they believed not in me.

10. And of justice: because I go to the Father: and you shall see me no longer.

11. And of judgment: because the prince of this world is already judged.

---

return. But our Lord had said explicitly where He was going (13: 36; 14: 5, 28), so the words can quite well mean: 'So (naturally) none of you asks Me where I am going, *but*, the fact of My departure fills you with grief. But it should not! It is to your advantage that I go away!'

7. Why was our Lord's departure and (apparently) the substitution of the Paraclete a good thing? Simply because if our Lord had remained for ever in His material presence upon earth, so astounding a miracle would have forced men to believe. But the whole scheme of Salvation is founded on faith. And His spiritual (and sacramental) presence, together with the indwelling of the Holy Spirit, must fully satisfy us.

8. 'Convict' rather than 'convince'. The 'world' means, immediately, the contemporary Jews, and, more remotely, all who culpably reject our Lord. The Holy Ghost, the 'Advocate' or supporter in a law-suit, turns 'Prosecutor': He impeaches and condemns the world in regard of sin (i.e. wilful disbelief in our Lord); in regard of righteousness (i.e. of not recognizing Him as the Righteous One: cf. Acts 3: 14; 22: 14; I Peter 3: 18); the words 'and you see Me no longer' do not add to the sense, but make a kind of complementary parallel with 'I go away to the Father': in regard of judgment, because the Jews will be proved wrong in condemning

The Paraclete will guide His disciples: 12–15

12. I have yet many things to say to you: but you cannot bear them now.

13. But when he, the Spirit of truth, is come, he will teach you all truth. For he shall not speak of himself: but what things soever he shall hear, he shall speak. And the things that are to come, he shall shew you.

14. He shall glorify me: because he shall receive of mine and shall shew *it* to you.

15. All things whatsoever the Father hath are mine. Therefore I said that he shall receive of mine and shew *it* to you.

'Ask, and you shall receive': 16–24

16. A little while, and now you shall not see me: and again a little while, and you shall see me: because I go to the Father.

17. Then some of his disciples said one to another: What is this that he saith to us: A little while, and you shall not see me; and again a little while, and you shall see me, and, Because I go to the Father?

Christ—it was they who stood convicted. The 'prince of this world' is already beaten—wounded to death—but still able to strike as a wounded snake can.

12. See on 15: 14. Till the Holy Ghost was given, the Apostles themselves could not 'fathom' our Lord's teaching, and were also able to receive new revelations till their death.

13. But the context implies that the further enlightenment was to be given after our Lord's departure: the Paraclete was to 'guide (them) into the whole truth' (*not* 'teach' as in Douai). The 'truth' into which the Spirit would lead them would not be a truth alien to that which Christ had taught, and which the Father had sent Him to teach. The prophecy about 'things to come' is insisted on in the Apocalypse 1: 19.

16, 17. 'Because I go to the Father' is not in the best MSS.: almost certainly our Lord refers to the interval between the crucifixion and the resurrection, not to that between the Ascension and the end of the world.

18. They said therefore: What is this that he saith, A little while? We know not what he speaketh.

19. And Jesus knew that they had a mind to ask him. And he said to them: Of this do you inquire among yourselves, because I said: A little while, and you shall not see me; and again a little while, and you shall see me?

20. Amen, amen, I say to you, that you shall lament and weep, but the world shall rejoice: and you shall be made sorrowful, but your sorrow shall be turned into joy.

21. A woman, when she is in labour, hath sorrow, because her hour is come; but when she hath brought forth the child, she remembereth no more the anguish, for joy that a man is born into the world.

22. So also you now indeed have sorrow: but I will see you again and your heart shall rejoice. And your joy no man shall take from you.

23. And in that day you shall not ask me any thing. Amen, amen, I say to you: if you ask the Father any thing in my name, he will give it you.

24. Hitherto, you have not asked any thing in my name. Ask, and you shall receive; that your joy may be full.

Jesus tells of His return to His Father: 25–33

25. These things I have spoken to you in proverbs. The hour cometh when I will no more speak to you in proverbs, but will shew you plainly of the Father.

---

21. The comparison with a woman suffering till her child is born, and then rejoicing, has no mystical significance. They will have a short space of sorrow, and then of a joy of which no human power can rob them.

23. It is unfortunate that Vg. translates both ἐρωτᾶν and αἰτεῖν by 'ask'. The first word means here that they will not have to *question* our Lord about anything; the latter, that they will be right to *ask*, and to do so 'in the name' of Jesus Christ, as we do.

25. 'Proverbs' is an unsuitable word: it now means on the whole

26. In that day, you shall ask in my name: and I say not to you that I will ask the Father himself for you.

27. For the Father himself loveth you, because you have loved me and have believed that I came out from God.

28. I came forth from the Father and am come into the world: again I leave the world and I go to the Father.

29. His disciples say to him: Behold, now thou speakest plainly and speaketh no proverb.

30. Now we know that thou knowest all things and thou needst not that any man should ask thee. By this we believe that thou camest forth from God.

---

an epigrammatic *sentence* with some moral significance which by long use has become 'proverbial'. Even 'parable' suggests a 'story' with a moral or other point, such as we read in the Synoptists. St John can hardly refer to the comparison with the vine, and the woman in labour, as characteristic of our Lord's teaching as he reports it. Our Lord's words and actions constantly held a meaning beyond the obvious one ('Destroy this temple, etc.': 'I would have given you living water': cf. the Loss and Finding in the Temple: the washing of the feet, the Ascension itself): nor did He alter His style of speaking after the Resurrection.

26. 'Ask' ($\dot{\epsilon}\rho\omega\tau\hat{a}\nu$) does not here mean 'question', but rather 'to ask the Father to attend to you': He does so already, 'because you love Me and believe in My divine origin'—however imperfect that faith still was. Yet our Lord still intercedes for us (Rom. 8: 34; Hebr. 7: 25; I John 2: 1): He, His Father, and the soul that believes and loves Him are intimately united, and our Lord, like the Holy Spirit, prays within us, as we pray not otherwise than in His name and person.

28. This verse is certainly plain speaking, yet the Apostles still had but a vague faith. 'I came forth out of God', is more clear than their response: 'Thou art come forth *from* God' in verse 30. It remains that the 'mystery' of the Blessed Trinity *cannot* be adequately expressed in human words; and however clearly

31. Jesus answered them: Do you now believe?

32. Behold, the hour cometh, and it is now come, that you shall be scattered every man to his own and shall leave me alone. And yet I am not alone, because the Father is with me.

33. These things I have spoken to you, that in me you may have peace. In the world you shall have distress. But have confidence. I have overcome the world.

---

the Apostles thought that our Lord spoke, and that they understood, they were still obliged to live by faith, and to pray.

32. 'Each to his own'; not, as usual, 'to his own house', but each would make off as best he could.

33. In spite of this, Jesus wishes the Apostles to keep peace within their hearts.

CHAPTER SEVENTEEN

Our Lord's Farewell Prayer (i): 1–10

1. These things Jesus spoke: and lifting up his eyes to heaven, he said: Father, the hour is come. Glorify thy Son, that thy Son may glorify thee.

2. As thou hast given him power over all flesh, that he may give eternal life to all whom thou hast given him.

3. Now this is eternal life: That they may know thee, the only true God, and Jesus Christ, whom thou hast sent.

4. I have glorified thee on the earth; I have finished the work which thou gavest me to do.

5. And now glorify thou me, O Father, with thyself, with the glory which I had, before the world was, with thee.

6. I have manifested thy name to the men whom thou hast given me out of the world. Thine they were: and to me thou gavest them. And they have kept thy word.

1–5. These verses form a separate prayer—for our Lord's own self. Our Lord's glory, and the glory He gives to His Father, will be the salvation of all men, if only they on their side 'keep God's word'.

3. This verse seems as it were an irresistible cry uttered by the Evangelist, if only because it is unnecessary that our Lord should explain to His Father what 'eternal life' is, but it is still more strange that He should name Himself 'Jesus Christ' (only here in the gospel save 1: 17, but often in St John's first and second epistles).

4. Not 'finished'; but 'accomplished': cf. 19: 30; 4: 34.

6. Doubtless our Lord has in mind all who throughout time shall be saved; but here He is praying specifically for those

7. Now they have known that all things which thou hast given me are from thee:

8. Because the words which thou gavest me, I have given to them. And they have received them and have known in very deed that I came out from thee: and they have believed that thou didst send me.

9. I pray for them. I pray not for the world, but for them whom thou hast given me: because they are thine.

10. And all my things are thine, and thine are mine: and I am glorified in them.

Our Lord's Farewell Prayer (ii): 11–19

11. And now I am not in the world, and these are in the world, and I come to thee. Holy Father, keep them in thy name whom thou hast given me: that they may be one, as we also are.

12. While I was with them, I kept them in thy name. Those whom thou gavest me have I kept: and none of them is lost, but the son of perdition, that the scripture may be fulfilled.

---

whom He had called and who had responded to Him because God had granted them the grace to do so. Cf. 6: 44, 65.

9. This makes it clear that He is praying definitely for the Apostles and not for the world at large: that will come later.

11. The word οὐκέτι, so often used, in verse 10 and here, means more than 'no longer'. 'But no longer (not "now") am I in the (i.e. this) world; they however *are* in the world, whereas I am going to Thee.' Verse 12 cannot be properly explained without reference to the Greek: the Douai version cannot be kept to.

12. 'In Thy name which Thou hast given to Me': not 'whom': (read, not οὕς but ᾧ) ᾧ is 'attracted' into the case of ὀνόματι: this would mean that the Father's authority is that too of the Son—they are 'one thing'—preserve them by Our power, so that they may be one thing, as We are. However, perhaps we should read ὅ, 'keep that which Thou hast given

13. And now I come to thee: and these things I speak in the world, that they may have my joy filled in themselves.

14. I have given them thy word, and the world hath hated them: because they are not of the world, as I also am not of the world.

15. I pray not that thou shouldst take them out of the world, but that thou shouldst keep them from evil.

16. They are not of the world, as I also am not of the world.

17. Sanctify them in truth. Thy word is truth.

18. As thou hast sent me into the world, I also have sent them into the world.

19. And for them do I sanctify myself, that they also may be sanctified in truth.

Me'; cf. verse 2. The neuter, ὅ, much emphasizes the closeness of the unity our Lord asks for His apostles: it was to reflect, in its way, the unity between Father and Son themselves. There is an assonance between ἀπώλετο, 'is lost', and ἀπωλείας, 'the son of loss', i.e. the man who would be lost; cf. Matt. 23: 15. We cannot echo the assonance better than by writing 'none of them has perished save the son of perdition': see Ps. 41: 10.

13. Our Lord's own joy is not 'fulfilled' till the hearts too of His friends are full of heavenly joy.

14–16. Our Lord has picked them out from the mass of men to be in a unique way His own: but He leaves them among those other men, asking only that they may not be infected by the evil which surrounds them—'the world's slow stain'.

17–19. Cf. 10: 36. The meaning of 'to sanctify' (ἁγιάζειν), is double: to 'set aside', but to set aside *for God*: the consecrated thing thus becomes 'holy', and can be offered as victim. Our Lord, thus consecrating Himself, acts as priest, and also, makes Himself a sacrifice. He does the same on behalf of His apostles, that they may participate in His role—'really', and not just metaphorically.

Our Lord's Farewell Prayer (iii): 20–26

20. And not for them only do I pray, but for them also who through their word shall believe in me.

21. That they all may be one, as thou, Father, in me, and I in thee; that they also may be one in us: that the world may believe that thou hast sent me.

22. And the glory which thou hast given me, I have given to them: that they may be one, as we also are one.

23. I in them, and thou in me: that they may be made perfect in one: and the world may know that thou hast sent me and hast loved them, as thou hast also loved me.

24. Father, I will that where I am, they also whom thou hast given me may be with me: that they may see my glory which thou hast given me, because thou hast loved me before the creation of the world.

25. Just Father, the world hath not known thee: but I have known thee. And these have known that thou hast sent me.

26. And I have made known thy name to them and will make it known: that the love wherewith thou hast loved me may be in them, and I in them.

---

20. The adhesion of faith is given to a Teaching, that doctrine taught by the Apostles which (Matt. 28: 20) is to continue for

21. ever; and the unity thus produced among believers is to provide a genuine motive for belief.

22, 23. Much rather than the exterior 'glory' due to the miracles worked by the Apostles and their successors, 'glory' here means that divine life which our Lord possesses as in its source along with the Father, and communicates to men so far as human nature is rendered able to receive it.

24. What has been given by the Father to the Son, belongs to the Son, who can therefore say what He wills should happen to it. And His will is, that they should be with Him and see the glory that was His in eternity, for the Father saw the Incarnation before the world existed, and loved what He saw. A kind of circulation of love is seen, between Father, Son, and the Saved.

CHAPTER EIGHTEEN

The Arrest: 1–11

(cf. Matt. 26: 47–56; Mark 14: 43–52; Luke 12: 47–53)

1. When Jesus had said these things, he went forth with his disciples over the brook Cedron, where there was a garden, into which he entered with his disciples.
2. And Judas also, who betrayed him, knew the place: because Jesus had often resorted thither together with his disciples.
3. Judas therefore having received a band of soldiers and servants from the chief priests and the Pharisees, cometh thither with lanterns and torches and weapons.

---

1. 'Went forth': from the house where they had supped. The 'brook' was probably at that season a dry torrent-bed. The Hebrew name for it, Qidron, means 'dark', 'black': the Greek Κέδρων is probably right: or κέδρων which would mean 'of the cedar(s)'. But Josephus who mentions the gully says nothing about cedars there. We do not think that John saw anything symbolic in the crossing of the dark ravine or any contrast between Gethsemani (named in Mark and Matt.) and Eden.
2. Perhaps our Lord had gone there nightly during Holy Week save on the first night of His coming to Jerusalem (Matt. 21: 17; Mark 11: 12): St Mark 11: 19 does not say where He went on leaving the City; St Luke speaks of the Mount of Olives (21: 37), His customary resort (22: 39).
3. A 'band' (σπεῖρα). Strictly, the third of a cohort, i.e. 200 men. No need to suppose that the whole garrison of the City, came, even though their officer is called (in verse 12) *chiliarchos*, captain of 1,000 men. The soldiers were naturally

4. Jesus therefore, knowing all things that should come upon him, went forth and said to them: Whom seek ye?

5. They answered him: Jesus of Nazareth. Jesus saith to them: I am he. And Judas also, who betrayed him, stood with them.

6. As soon therefore as he had said to them: I am he; they went backward and fell to the ground.

7. Again therefore he asked them: Whom seek ye? And they said: Jesus of Nazareth.

8. Jesus answered: I have told you that I am he. If therefore you seek me, let these go their way,

9. That the word might be fulfilled which he said: Of them whom thou hast given me, I have not lost any one.

10. Then Simon Peter, having a sword, drew it and struck the servant of the high priest and cut off his right ear. And the name of the servant was Malchus.

---

sent, since it was seen that a crowd of Jews was surging out and liable to create trouble. The Jewish police needed supervision as badly as the mob. Cf. Mark, 15: 16.

4. 'Knowing': practically 'though He knew'. 'Came out': whence? from the garden? Probably, from the place whither He had withdrawn to pray.

5. There may be contempt in the use of 'the Nazarene' (cf. 19: 19; Matt. 26: 71): 'from Nazareth' would be more natural. 'I am He'. In Greek, simply 'I am': the Name of God. The Romans would not have perceived this: possibly the Jews, in front, did so, were horrified by the words and maybe a sense of divine majesty inspired by the personality of our Lord, staggered back and caused the confusion described in verse 6.

8, 9. His second assertion that He was the one they were looking for, was intended to give the Apostles the chance of escaping: 'Of those that Thou hast given me, etc.' occur in 17: 12; but there they allude to spiritual loss: St John recalls them here, where our Lord does not wish His disciples (whom He calls merely 'these men') to be involved in His arrest.

10, 11. John adds the name of the servant: *the* servant of the high-

11. Jesus therefore said to Peter: Put up thy sword into the scabbard. The chalice which my father hath given me, shall I not drink it?

Our Lord before Annas: 12–14

12. Then the band and the tribune and the servants of the Jews took Jesus and bound him.

13. And they led him away to Annas first, for he was father-in-law to Caiaphas, who was the high priest of that year.

14. Now Caiaphas was he who had given the counsel to the Jews: That it was expedient that one man should die for the people.

---

priest implies that he was the leader of the Temple-police. Our Lord had prayed (Mark 14: 36 and parallels) that the chalice of His Passion should be removed from Him, if possible: but it became clear that His Father's will was that He should 'drink' it, He expresses here His perfect acceptance of that divine will.

13. If Caiaphas was high-priest, why go to Annas? The office of high-priest was held for life: but the Romans easily removed a man they objected to and substituted another. Annas therefore was strictly speaking 'high-priest', and at least a visit of courtesy was felt to be due to him. Caiaphas, as 'acting high-priest', would preside at the actual trial. But 'of that year'? No one supposed that the high-priesthood was an annual office: St John must mean 'of *that* year—that unique year' when our Lord was crucified. Caiaphas was high-priest from about A.D. 18–36. Annas had been deposed about A.D. 15, and though remaining influential had no legal position. It is said that the Romans put the high-priest's office up to annual auction, managing always to get a man they approved of into that position, and that Caiaphas, by 'good behaviour' retained it for so long. But St John will hardly have written of a scandalous fact as if it were normal and outside of criticism.

Peter's First Denial of our Lord: 15–18

15. And Simon Peter followed Jesus: and so did another disciple. And that disciple was known to the high priest and went in with Jesus into the court of the high priest.

16. But Peter stood at the door without. The other disciple therefore, who was known to the high priest, went out and spoke to the portress and brought in Peter.

17. The maid therefore that was portress saith to Peter: Art not thou also one of this man's disciples? He saith: I am not.

18. Now the servants and ministers stood at a fire of coals, because it was cold, and warmed themselves. And with them was Peter also, standing, and warming himself.

Jesus Answers the High Priest: 19–24

19. The high priest therefore asked Jesus of his disciples and of his doctrine.

---

15. The other disciple is not named, but no one save St John can be suggested. He was sufficiently well known to Caiaphas to be known also to the servants;

16. St John had only to say that he wanted to bring a friend in with him: it may be surprising that the person in charge of the door was a woman; St John does not give every detail—maybe the usual door-keeper had run in with the crowd and had left a maid-servant in charge for the moment.

17. 'Surely you too are not one of this man's disciples?' That is, as well as St John. This seems to be the only explanation of why she put the question at all.

18. The servants and assistants 'had taken their stand' round a fire that they 'had been making' (pluperfect and perfect verbs): presumably they had gone straight to Caiaphas's house without visiting Annas: Peter was standing with them. Matthew and Luke say he was seated: the point was that he was *with* the others, doing as they did. Presumably some stood, some sat or squatted at least part of the time.

20. Jesus answered him: I have spoken openly to the world. I have always taught in the synagogue and in the temple, whither all the Jews resort: and in secret I have spoken nothing.
21. Why asketh thou me? Ask them who have heard what I have spoken unto them. Behold they know what things I have said.
22. And when he had said these things, one of the servants standing by gave Jesus a blow, saying: Answereth thou the high priest so?
23. Jesus answered him: If I have spoken evil, give testimony of the evil; but if well, why strikest thou me?
24. And Annas sent him bound to Caiaphas the high priest.

Peter's Second and Third Denials: 25–27

25. And Simon Peter was standing and warming himself. They said therefore to him: Art not thou also one of his disciples? He denied it and said: I am not.

20, 21. Our Lord had of course had private conversations (cf. Nicodemus; or in the Supper-room); but He had not preached any secret doctrine—even of His divinity He had spoken openly (10: 30, 38). The Synoptists place this statement of our Lord's at the time of His arrest: it would be suitable in both places: in each case He was held as prisoner, with no charge laid against Him.

22, 23. It is impossible that throughout this episode 'high-priest' should be used of Annas, and then of Caiaphas, without qualification: this is one reason why we think verse 24 is out of place and should follow 13.

25. Peter was evidently where he was before. But if his first denial had been in Annas's house, he would have left it in order to follow our Lord to Caiaphas, unless we assume (with no evidence) that Annas and Caiaphas shared a house and had, e.g., a courtyard in common. According to Matthew and Mark the second denial took place near the door: St Luke seems to place an hour between the second and third denial. It is possible that Peter, amid the tumult of the courtyard,

26. One of the servants of the high priest (a kinsman to him whose ear Peter cut off) saith to him: Did not I see thee in the garden with him?

27. Again therefore Peter denied: and immediately the cock crew.

Our Lord before Pilate: 28–32

28. Then they led Jesus from Caiaphas to the governor's hall. And it was morning: and they went not into the hall, that they might not be defiled, but that they might eat the pasch.

29. Pilate therefore went out to them, and said: What accusation bring you against this man?

30. They answered and said to him: If he were not a malefactor, we would not have delivered him up to thee.

---

repeated his denial several times: but, as our Lord definitely said (according to all the Synoptists) that Peter would deny Him thrice, it is probable that John wished to emphasize the triple denial rather than to state exactly when and where it took place.

28. We may think that here John aims at supplementing the Synoptists by relating more fully what happened in the presence of Pilate, while omitting what was so well known—the earlier 'trial' and condemnation by the sanhedrists. We should read: '*Therefore* they led Jesus from Caiaphas's. . . .' He had been condemned to death for blasphemy, but it was the Governor who alone could give legal effect to the sentence. The 'praetorium' was the residence of the Governor when in Jerusalem: it may have been the fortress at the N.W. of the city, or, Herod's palace on the western hill. St John makes it clear that this was Friday, Nisan 14th, on which the Pasch must be eaten. Now the Synoptists make it no less clear that our Lord treated the Last Supper as His own Pasch. For explanations of this, see Notes upon the synoptic gospels.

It was only a 'tradition', not part of the Law, that entry into a pagan's house caused ritual pollution.

31. Pilate therefore said to them: Take him you, and judge him according to your law. The Jews therefore said to him: It is not lawful for us to put any man to death.

32. That the word of Jesus might be fulfilled, which he said, signifying what death he should die.

'What is Truth?': 33-40

33. Pilate therefore went into the hall again and called Jesus and said to him: Art thou the king of the Jews?

34. Jesus answered: Sayest thou this thing of thyself, or have others told it thee of me?

---

30. Pilate had asked a formal question: the Jews' reply can hardly have been a mere piece of impertinence: they took it for granted that Pilate had heard at least in outline that Jesus had been condemned on religious grounds, and rightly so.

31. Pilate implies that such matters are outside his competence; let them settle their own religious differences. This brings them into the open: they cannot legally execute a man: but if Pilate ordered the execution, this would be done by crucifixion— had the Jews, in a rage, killed a man, it would have been by stoning (cf. St Stephen: Acts 7: 58). Now our Lord had often said He would be crucified (in John, see 3: 14; 12: 2). In these episodes, remember (a) that John writes only the necessary outline of events and (b) that this 'trial' was not conducted in the orderly, even chilly way in which ours are, when any disturbance in court is instantly checked, but in the midst of a clamour of infuriated men who hated the Judge almost as much as they did the Prisoner.

33. Pilate went 'back' into the house, not 'again'. He had come to a window or the head of a flight of steps. His question shows that he had caught some suggestion of a political aspect in this tumult, unless John is omitting as much as he can to reach the dialogue within.

34. Our Lord asks in what sense the question is put to him—in one

35. Pilate answered: Am I a Jew? Thy own nation and the chief priests have delivered thee up to me. What hast thou done?

36. Jesus answered: My kingdom is not of this world. If my kingdom were of this world, my servants would certainly strive that I should not be delivered to the Jews: but now my kingdom is not from hence.

37. Pilate therefore said to him: Art thou a king then? Jesus answered: Thou sayest that I am a king. For this was I born, and for this came I into the world; that I should give testimony to the truth. Every one that is of the truth heareth my voice.

38. Pilate saith to him: What is truth? And when he said this, he went out again to the Jews and saith to them: I find no cause in him.

39. But you have a custom that I should release one unto you at the pasch. Will you, therefore, that I release unto you the king of the Jews?

40. Then cried they all again, saying: Not this man, but Barabbas. Now Barabbas was a robber.

---

sense He is indeed king of the Jews: in Pilate's sense, He is not claiming to be king at all.

35. Pilate is irritated: it is not *he* who sets going quarrels such as these! Of course the Jews started it! He is there to keep the peace.

36. Our Lord says He is not king at all in the worldly sense: why, the Jews are actually His enemies: He has no partisans to fight for Him.

37. 'So then you *are* a king (in some sense)?' Jesus now says positively that He *is*—that He was born and entered the world to proclaim the Truth, and that all who were 'of the truth', had ears open to it, would understand His message.

38. Pilate was an official, not a speculative philosopher. The Empire was full of theorists whom the Government could disregard unless they disturbed the public peace. So he went out and said that he found no reason why Jesus should be condemned.

39, 40. Pilate therefore should simply have set Jesus free: in Mark, 15: 6 it is the Jews who first demand Barabbas: here Pilate, with a sneer, says 'there is a custom of yours' . . . and then asks simply if they would like 'the king of the Jews' to be freed. Another sneer, amply sufficient to exasperate the Jews and make them choose Barabbas. John's curt: 'Now Barabbas was a robber' (a man of violence and bloodshed) is even more telling than the longer explanations of the Synoptists.

CHAPTER NINETEEN

The Scourging: the Crowning: the 'Ecce Homo': 1–16

1. Then therefore Pilate took Jesus and scourged him.
2. And the soldiers platting a crown of thorns, put it upon his head: and they put on him a purple garment.
3. And they came to him and said: Hail, king of the Jews. And they gave him blows.
4. Pilate therefore went forth again and saith to them: Behold, I bring him forth unto you, that you may know that I find no cause in him.
5. (Jesus therefore came forth, bearing the crown of thorns and the purple garment.) And he saith to them: Behold the Man.
6. When the chief priests, therefore, and the servants had seen him, they cried out, saying: Crucify him, Crucify him. Pilate saith to them: Take him you, and crucify him: for I find no cause in him.

---

1. The Synoptists place the scourging and mock crowning after the condemnation, which would certainly be in accordance with Roman custom. St Luke however (23: 4, 14, 16) mentions Pilate's triple declaration that Jesus was not worthy of death; we may suppose that Pilate (who was not scrupulous about legal forms) thought that though the Jews had demanded the liberation of Barabbas and the crucifixion of Jesus, they would be satisfied if the former were in fact set free, and if Jesus were scourged, while his own conscience would not be troubled by a flagrant injustice, i.e. having condemned Him to death. The crowning with thorns was not ordered by Pilate, but was a brutal sport invented by the soldiers directly after the scourging.

4, 5. Pilate produced our Lord in his pitiable condition, not as proclaiming Him innocent, but as showing that there was no need to go further, and to put Him to death.

146

7. The Jews answered him: We have a law; and according to the law he ought to die, because he made himself the Son of God.

8. When Pilate therefore had heard this saying, he feared the more.

9. And he entered into the hall again; and he said to Jesus: Whence art thou? But Jesus gave him no answer.

10. Pilate therefore saith to him: Speakest thou not to me? Knowest thou not that I have power to crucify thee, and I have power to release thee?

11. Jesus answered: Thou shouldst not have any power against me, unless it were given thee from above. Therefore, he that hath delivered me to thee hath the greater sin.

6, 7. But the priests and their attendants cried still louder for crucifixion; Pilate is getting angry—'Take *you* Him. . . . *I* find no cause in Him'. The pronouns are emphatic: the Jews recognize that the words were a disdainful jest, but obstinately appeal to their law (Lev. 24: 16) and declare that Jesus had claimed to be God.

8, 9. Pilate was '*still more* frightened'. But we have not yet been told that he was frightened at all. Possibly John knows (but has not said) that Pilate was already 'nervous'—distracted by his dislike for an obvious injustice, and by his fear of a riot and of trouble in Rome. Perhaps too the message sent by his wife had stirred the superstitious element within him (Matt. 27: 19). His question: 'Whence art thou?' implies a suspicion that there might be something supernatural about his origin (see on ἄνωθεν, p. 23). Jesus does not answer: Pilate had shown he was at least as sceptic as sincere at heart.

10, 11. Pilate is now exasperated: '*Me* . . . you don't answer *me*?' Ἐμοί makes it very emphatic. The claim to 'power' need not imply claim to *absolute* power. He means that the final decision, once the facts are known, rests with *him*. Our Lord says Pilate would have *no* power (i.e. to put Him to death) were it not providentially given him by God (cf. 3: 3, only here there could be no ambiguity about the meaning of the word). Pilate was comparatively guiltless, because though in

12. And from henceforth Pilate sought to release him. But the Jews cried out, saying: If thou release this man, thou art not Cæsar's friend. For whosoever making himself a king speaketh against Cæsar.

13. Now when Pilate had heard these words, he brought Jesus forth and sat down in the judgment seat, in the place that is called Lithostrotos, and in Hebrew Gabbatha.

14. And it was the parasceve of the pasch, about the sixth hour: and he saith to the Jews: Behold your king.

---

his heart he thought our Lord politically innocent, he had not engineered His betrayal, arrest and prosecution as the others had.

12. Either 'from that moment', or, 'because of this' ($\dot{\epsilon}\kappa$ $\tau o\acute{\upsilon}\tau o\upsilon$): Pilate felt not only that our Lord was innocent, but he was uncertain whether there might not be something super-natural about Him. Pilate's attitude has changed. So far, he has said only that he does not see why he should condemn Jesus. Now he positively wishes to release Him. The Jews play their last card, abdicating even their claim to national liberty:'Even though Christ's pretence to kingship be preposterous, it *is* a "pretence", and therefore criminal. If you condone it, you are not a "friend" of Caesar's. All pretence to kingship is "anti-Caesar".' The term 'friend of Caesar' was not exactly official; but the least suggestion of disloyalty was almost certainly fatal. This made Pilate brush aside all other considerations.

13. 'Sat down': the Greek $\dot{\epsilon}\kappa\acute{a}\theta\iota\sigma\epsilon\nu$ *can* be transitive; but it is absurd to suppose that Pilate, even in derision, caused Jesus to sit down on the official chair. *Lithostrotos* was a name given to any paved area: we cannot tell why this particular space or yard acquired that name: *Gabbatha* is what the Jews called it and is not an equivalent of Lithostrotos. Its meaning is quite conjectural.

14. St John defines the day and hour—'*about*' the 6th hour, i.e. noon. Cf. notes on Mark 15: 25 who puts the actual crucifixion at the third hour. Pilate presents Jesus a second time in

15. But they cried out: Away with him: Away with him: Crucify him. Pilate saith to them: Shall I crucify your king? The chief priests answered: We have no king but Cæsar.

16. Then therefore he delivered him to them to be crucified. And they took Jesus and led him forth.

The Crucifixion: 17–22

17. And bearing his own cross, he went forth to that place which is called Calvary, but in Hebrew Golgotha.

18. Where they crucified him, and with him two others, one on each side, and Jesus in the midst.

19. And Pilate wrote a title also: and he put it upon the cross. And the writing was: JESUS OF NAZARETH, THE KING OF THE JEWS.

20. This title therefore many of the Jews did read: because the place where Jesus was crucified was nigh to the city. And it was written in Hebrew, in Greek, and in Latin.

His pitiable state, and says with bitter sarcasm: 'There's your king!'

15. To the reiterated cries Pilate answers: 'Shall I crucify *your* King?' The chief priests say what the populace, even maddened, would not have dared to: 'We have no king but Caesar.' Then Pilate hands Him over.

17. This does not contradict the story of the Cyrenian. First, criminals *had* to carry their own cross: our Lord will have started by doing so and when clearly too exhausted to go on, He had to be helped. The place is as in the Synoptists, save that St John naturally puts the Latin name first.

18. 'They crucified Him', i.e. the soldiers. St John merely alludes to the two thieves, about whom St Luke had said enough, exquisite though the story be.

19. St John alone uses the equivalent of the Latin *titulus*— ($\tau\iota\tau\lambda o\varsigma$). The three Synoptists have 'King of the Jews'; St Matthew adds 'Jesus', and St John further adds 'from Nazareth', especially irritating at Jerusalem.

20. The three languages were those of officialdom (Latin), of the

21. Then the chief priests of the Jews said to Pilate: Write not: The King of the Jews. But that he said: I am the King of the Jews.

22. Pilate answered: What I have written, I have written.

The Consummation: 23–30

23. The soldiers therefore, when they had crucified him, took his garments, (and they made four parts, to every soldier a part) and also his coat. Now the coat was without seam, woven from the top throughout.

24. They said then one to another: Let us not cut it, but let us cast lots for it, whose it shall be; that the scripture might be fulfilled, saying: *They have parted my garments among them, and upon my vesture they have cast lots.*[1] And the soldiers indeed did these things.

25. Now there stood by the cross of Jesus, his mother and his mother's sister, Mary of Cleophas, and Mary Magdalen.

26. When Jesus therefore had seen his mother and the disciple standing whom he loved, he saith to his mother: Woman, behold thy son.

27. After that, he saith to the disciple: Behold thy mother. And from that hour, the disciple took her to his own.

---

educated (Greek), and (Aramaic) of the common people. Many inscriptions in at any rate two languages survive.

21, 22. Pilate is now obstinate: what he has written, is written once for all.

23, 24. The Synoptists do not refer to Ps. 21: 19: the psalm says nothing about 'without seam', and the two parts of the verse refer to the same action, namely, that lots were cast for the Psalmist's clothes. The double action of the soldiers *recalls* the psalm to St John without implying that it was an accurate prediction: it is known that the high-priest wore a robe made of a single piece which would have been spoilt by cutting it.

25–27. With the exception of our Lady, the women are the same as those mentioned by the Synoptists, since Salome is presumably the same as the mother of the sons of Zebedee

[1] Psalm 21: 19.

28. Afterwards, Jesus knowing that all things were now accomplished, that the scripture might be fulfilled, said: I thirst.

29. Now there was a vessel set there, full of vinegar. And they, putting a sponge full of vinegar about hyssop, put it to his mouth.

They are however there said to have stood at a distance. But it is natural to suppose that (especially as the crowds thinned— owing to the coming on of darkness, and even to curiosity satisfied) St John brought our Lady and one or two others to the foot of the cross. The entrusting of His Mother to St John and of St John to her is perfectly simple in itself: we may add that Mary being the Mother of Christ Himself, is therefore the Mother of His mystical Body too, for our Lord does not consider Himself complete without His Christians. Origen already said that since Christ lives in the 'perfect' (in those, we should say, to whom unifying grace is granted), Mary is told that they too are her sons. 'To his own': a vague term; perhaps his mother's house: perhaps he went back to Galilee: 'from that hour' cannot here mean more than 'afterwards': as if either Mary or John could have tolerated to leave Jesus to die alone upon His cross! Further, while we do not think that this episode happened just before His death, we think that what follows did happen soon before it, and that John was still eye-witness.

28, 29. It is said that those who suffer such agony as our Lord's, especially with great loss of blood, may feel desperately thirsty: our Lord expressed His thirst, and St John recalls the words in Ps. 68: 22: 'Unto my thirst they gave me vinegar to drink.' The action there is an unkindly one: not so here, or in Mark 15: 36 or Matt. 27: 48 (Luke is briefer), where it follows closely on our Lord's cry 'Eli, Eli'. The 'vinegar' is the *posca*, the sharp wine drunk by soldiers or the poor: a sponge was often used as stopper for flasks. St Matthew and St Mark say that it was placed on a reed or cane: St John says on a hyssop: all three use the same verb for 'to put around' ($\pi\epsilon\rho\iota\tau\iota\theta\acute{\epsilon}\nu\alpha\iota$). Now hyssop is a weak-stemmed plant and could not support

30. Jesus therefore, when he had taken the vinegar, said: It is consummated. And bowing his head, he gave up the ghost.

---

a sponge soaked in liquid nor could a sponge be 'put around' hyssop-leaves. I cannot but accept an emendation proposed long ago by the writer Camerarius (d. 1574): the original text will have read νσσωιπεριθεντες 'putting it round a 'hyssos' (ὕσσος)', or short javelin: now ὕσσος is a rare word, and a copyist can easily have written νσσωπῳπεριθεντες either because ὕσσωπος would have been familiar to him, or by accident because of the similarity of the syllables: St John, watching from close by, could have seen just what happened: an eye-witness, but at a greater distance, would have seen simply some sort of rod. We can thus form an idea of the height of our Lord's mouth above the ground.

30. 'It is consummated' is the right translation of the Greek τετέλεσται and not 'It is finished', nor, we think, 'It is achieved' (Mgr Knox): perhaps we have no word for expressing the idea that a long task has been brought to completeness; not merely has the highest point been reached, the past being left behind, but all the long past has been preserved; all the promises kept and the prophecies fulfilled in and by our Lord. We think that it was just before our Lord 'inclined His head' that He spoke the words recorded by St Luke: 'Father, into Thy hands I commend my spirit' (23: 46), or else, just before St John's 'It has been made perfect—full-filled'. Once again, the Evangelists were not writing a *biography* of Christ; and St John in particular was not recording every single detail that he remembered, but wished to prove our Lord's divinity by what he selected. He may here and there have deliberately added what Synoptists omitted (e.g. the presence of our Lady by the Cross) or have omitted what he felt was known to the early Christians practically by heart. And certainly he did not mean to insist on all the harrowing details of the Crucifixion, much as *we* would have loved to know every detail about our Lord;

The Piercing of the Side: 31–37

31. Then the Jews (because it was the parasceve), that the bodies might not remain upon the cross on the sabbath day (for that was a great sabbath day), besought Pilate that their legs might be broken: and that they might be taken away.

32. The soldiers therefore came: and they broke the legs of the first, and of the other that was crucified with him.

33. But after they were come to Jesus, when they saw that he was already dead, they did not break his legs.

34. But one of the soldiers with a spear opened his side: and immediately there came out blood and water.

35. And he that saw it hath given testimony: and his testimony is true. And he knoweth that he saith true: that you also may believe.

36. For these things were done that the scripture might be fulfilled: *You shall not break a bone of him.*[1]

37. And again another scripture saith: *They shall look on him whom they pierced.*[2]

---

he wishes us to see the saving Death itself as part of the final enduring triumph.

31. Dt. 21: 23 decrees that the body of an executed man must be buried the same day: this was still the custom in our Lord's time when a man had been crucified. But the Jews wished to make sure that the three victims were dead, lest the removal of their bodies should infringe the Sabbath, especially as *that* Sabbath was also Nisan 15th, the beginning of the paschal feasts.

32. The *crurifragium* was a brutal but frequent penalty inflicted on e.g. runaway slaves: it was thought that it would suffice to make an end of men already exhausted by pain.

34-37. One soldier however determined to make sure that Jesus was dead, and clearly aimed at the heart with his long lance. The 'blood and water' may have been due to the separation of the red element in blood from the colourless serum: but the point

[1] Exod. 12: 46; Num. 9: 12.   [2] Zach. 12: 10.

The Burial: 38–42

38. And after these things, Joseph of Arimathea (because he was a disciple of Jesus, but secretly for fear of the Jews), besought Pilate that he might take away the body of Jesus. And Pilate gave leave. He came therefore and took away the body of Jesus.

39. And Nicodemus also came (he who at the first came to Jesus by night), bringing a mixture of myrrh and aloes, about an hundred pound *weight*.

---

is, that the event both proved that Jesus was dead, and also has a mystical value. Else St John would not have insisted so much on his being an eye-witness of it. We think it possible that the words 'and his testimony is true, and he knows that he tells the truth' may have been added by an assistant of the Evangelist's, insisting that St John cannot possibly be wrong. But it has been argued that '*he* knows, etc.' may allude to our Lord: ἐκεῖνος is an emphatic pronoun and does so allude in John 2: 6; 3: 3, 5, 7, 16. The historical event has been the basis for symbolical interpretations; but St John does not himself make any here: he does however see the fulfilment of two prophecies; Num. 9: 12, about the paschal lamb whose bones were not to be broken; and Zach. 12: 10, 'they shall look to me whom they have pierced'. The original bearing of the Hebrew may be obscure: but in the actual piercing of our Lord's side St John sees the words realized, and quotes them again in Apoc. 1: 7. Men's eyes turn towards the sacrificed Son of God, and they may either foresee in Him their own condemnation, or, their salvation.

38, 39. Pilate had already (verse 31) ordered that the bodies should be removed: but either Joseph did not know this, or he made use of his position, mentioned by the Synoptists, to make a special request to Pilate that *he* should carry out the removal. There was no time to lose: Nicodemus undertook to buy the spices. The amount seems so enormous that it seems possible that the numeral is due to an early copyist's fault. In any case,

40. They took therefore the body of Jesus and bound it in linen cloths, with the spices, as the manner of the Jews is to bury.

41. Now there was in the place where he was crucified a garden: and in the garden a new sepulchre, wherein no man yet had been laid.

42. There, therefore, because of the parasceve of the Jews, they laid Jesus: because the sepulchre was nigh at hand.

---

myrrh (very likely almost powdery) and aloes (little twigs, or tied into bundles) were not used for the regular embalming of a dead body: the women proposed to do this more fully when the sabbath was over, assuming indeed that they knew what had already been done.

41. We must not picture a garden like ours: it will have been a walled enclosure, with some trees and maybe plants, and a place where entry into a tomb could be made.

CHAPTER TWENTY

The Empty Tomb (i): *Peter and John: 1–10*

1. And on the first day of the week, Mary Magdalen cometh early, when it was yet dark, unto the sepulchre: and she saw the stone taken away from the sepulchre.

2. She ran therefore and cometh to Simon Peter and to the other disciple whom Jesus loved and saith to them: They have taken away the Lord out of the sepulchre: and we know not where they have laid him.

3. Peter therefore went out, and that other disciple: and they came to the sepulchre.

4. And they both ran together: and that other disciple did outrun Peter and came first to the sepulchre.

5. And when he stooped down he saw the linen cloths lying: but yet he went not in.

6. Then cometh Simon Peter, following him, and went into the sepulchre: and saw the linen cloths lying,

---

1, 2. John mentions only the Magdalen because of what he will relate in a moment, but verse 2, 'we', shows that he remembers the presence of others; all the Synoptists mention Magdalen. Mark 16: 2 says that the women arrived when the sun was risen; Luke 24: 1 says it was 'very early'. Matt. 28: 1 that it was beginning to dawn. It may well be that Magdalen hurried ahead of the rest, saw the stone removed, concluded that the Body was taken away and ran back to tell the apostles, having heard no more than the cries of the other women who had looked into the tomb and seen the angels.

3–5. John outruns Peter, being the younger; but Peter enters first, being the more impetuous.

6, 7. He 'looks at' (θεωρεῖ)—more than just 'sees': almost

156

7. And the napkin that had been about his head, not lying with the linen cloths, but apart, wrapped up into one place.

8. Then that other disciple also went in, who came first to the sepulchre: and he saw and believed.

9. For as yet they knew not the scripture, that he must rise again from the dead.

10. The disciples therefore departed again to their home.

The Empty Tomb (ii) : Mary Magdalen: 11–18

11. But Mary stood at the sepulchre without, weeping. Now as she was weeping, she stooped down and looked into the sepulchre,

12. And she saw two angels in white, sitting, one at the head, and one at the feet, where the body of Jesus had been laid.

13. They say to her: Woman, why weepest thou? She saith to them: Because they have taken away my Lord; and I know not where they have laid him.

'examines'. The linen bandages which had wrapped the body lay flat, as they were: but a separate cloth which had been put round the head was rolled up, separately, and by itself.

8–10. 'He believed'; i.e. that the Body was no more there (i.e. as Magdalen had said: so, St Augustine). St John says definitely that 'they' did not 'know', i.e. understand, realize, the Scripture, that He must rise. As if our Lord Himself had not insisted that He would! It is not only the Synoptists who dwell on the inability of the disciples to admit so amazing an occurrence!

11. Mary, we think, had come back to the tomb, but more slowly than the apostles: she was tired by having run, and by violent emotion: still, she could not keep away from the tomb and kept her place there even when the other two went back.

12, 13. She went on weeping and peering into the tomb (imperfects) and then had her vision of angels—John indicates their position: our Lord had been laid on a stone ledge; possibly there was a support for the head as has been found in other

14. When she had thus said, she turned herself back and saw Jesus standing: and she knew not that it was Jesus.

15. Jesus saith to her: Woman, why weepest thou? Whom seekest thou? She, thinking that it was the gardener, saith to him: Sir, if thou hast taken him hence, tell me where thou hast laid him: and I will take him away.

16. Jesus saith to her: Mary. She turning, saith to him: Rabboni (which is to say, Master).

17. Jesus said to her: Do not touch me: for I am not yet ascended to my Father. But go to my brethren and say to them: I ascend to my Father and to your Father, to my God and to your God.

18. Mary Magdalen cometh and telleth the disciples: I have seen the Lord; and these things he said to me.

---

such tombs. 'I know not' shows that the others had gone away.

14–16. She turns back to find Him, perhaps, elsewhere, since He is not here. We think that our Lord avoided too great a shock to her, by a *gradual* approach to manifesting Himself alive. Mary, absorbed in her unhappiness and her eyes full of tears and her thought wholly preoccupied, assumes that the half-seen figure is the gardener. No doubt our Lord may have 'disguised' Himself, cf. Luke 24: 16; Mark 16: 12: the glorified spirit can control the flesh: but perhaps this is not necessary. In desperation she asks to be told where he has placed Him, *if* it is he who has removed Him—and then *she* will carry Him away—never reflecting how, or whither. He needs but to speak her name, in the voice that reaches her heart, and with one word she answers. '*My* Master!' (*Rabboni*) expresses not only reverence but a possessive love.

17, 18. 'Do not lay hold of (or cling to) Me: I have not yet ascended to my Father, but . . .' We think that this sentence contains a double sense: first, our Lord lovingly tells her not to cling thus passionately to Him—He is still here; He is not about to vanish: then, that none the less, she must go and tell 'His brothers' (He does not here use the usual and less

The Apparition to Ten Disciples: 19–23

19. Now when it was late that same day, the first of the week, and the doors were shut, where the disciples were gathered together, for fear of the Jews, Jesus came and stood in the midst and said to them: Peace be to you.

20. And when he had said this, he shewed them his hands and his side. The disciples therefore were glad, when they saw the Lord.

21. He said therefore to them again: Peace be to you. As the Father hath sent me, I also send you.

22. When he had said this, he breathed on them; and he said to them: Receive ye the Holy Ghost.

23. Whose sins you shall forgive, they are forgiven them: and whose *sins* you shall retain, they are retained.

---

affectionate term 'disciples') that He is indeed risen but will not be with them always. For her, there is still plenty of time: but for them, days were few. Much 'training' had to be carried through in a short space. Also, looking further ahead, the Christian must associate with our Lord wholly by faith, not sight. Yet how close is the association implied by 'My Father and your Father—My God and your God'!

19. The shut doors could not have kept out a deliberate attack; but the disciples wished to exclude anyone not of their group. Also, the point is that our Lord's entrance was supernatural in regard of *them*; cf. Luke 24: 31. 'Peace to you!' was a usual Jewish salutation, but acquired a fuller meaning after the terrible hours through which they had passed, and, His abrupt apparition would cause fear at first.

20. In showing His presence corporally thus, He could show also His wounds, not in reproach, but as proof that it was indeed Himself, and, that the Passion was *over*. St John hastens as usual to doctrine, and does not mention our Lord's eating with them, as St Luke does, 24: 42, 43.

21–23. Luke 24: 49, speaks of the promise of the Holy Spirit, to be fulfilled at Pentecost: this act is clearly different from that

The Apparition to Thomas: 24–31

24. Now Thomas, one of the twelve, who is called Didymus, was not with them when Jesus came.

25. The other disciples therefore said to him: We have seen the Lord. But he said to them: Except I shall see in his hands the print of the nails and put my finger into the place of the nails and put my hand into his side, I will not believe.

26. And after eight days, again his disciples were within, and Thomas with them. Jesus cometh, the doors being shut, and stood in the midst and said: Peace be to you.

27. Then he saith to Thomas: Put in thy finger hither and see my hands. And bring hither thy hand and put it into my side. And be not faithless, but believing.

28. Thomas answered and said to him: My Lord and my God.

29. Jesus saith to him: Because thou hast seen me, Thomas, thou hast believed: blessed are they that have not seen and have believed.

Mission of the Paraclete which was to replace our Lord's bodily presence (John 14: 16, 26; 16: 7, 13). His breath *is* not the Holy Spirit, but symbolizes Him, and our Lord in fact imparts Him: this gift had already been made, cf. Matt. 16: 19; 18: 18; but either to Peter personally or in more general terms, though the Council of Trent says that it is 'now especially that the sacrament of penance was instituted': the conditions for its use are laid down by the Church; but what is essential, contrition, and resolve to do the 'works of God', is clear from the whole of our Lord's teaching.

24. In 14: 5 we see a certain obstinacy in Thomas; he wants our Lord to be more explicit. But in 11: 16 we see the generous side of him. His absence may be due to an almost despairing sorrow; and to this, also, the all-but brutality of the condition he lays down for belief.

26–29. '8 days', i.e. counting the present day as the first, as in French. Thomas's reply is not a pure exclamation (like Magdalen's Rabboni) which would have required a vocative;

An Epilogue: 30–31

30. Many other signs also did Jesus in the sight of his disciples, which are not written in this book.

31. But these are written, that you may believe that Jesus is the Christ, the Son of God: and that believing, you may have life in his name.

---

but, rather, a profession of faith: '(Thou art) my Lord and my God!' Perhaps our Lord's answer is a question: 'Is it because you have *seen* Me that you have believed?' The last words look forward to those who, like ourselves, have no chance of 'seeing': we have our special blessing.

30, 31. This certainly sounds like the conclusion of a book. But then, what of the next chapter? It seems to us entirely in the style of St John, but it has its own 'epilogue', verses 24 and 25. Some think it possible that verses 30 and 31 occurred after 21: 23, for to end that chapter at 23 would be very abrupt. Here, anyhow, St John has made his purpose quite clear: he has selected certain events and discourses of our Lord's in order to make still firmer the faith of those who believed already, or, perhaps, were hesitating as to faith: cf. 1 John 5: 13.

CHAPTER TWENTY-ONE

The Apparition by the Lake of Galilee: 1–14

1. After this, Jesus shewed himself again to the disciples at the sea of Tiberias. And he shewed *himself* after this manner.

2. There were together: Simon Peter and Thomas, who is called Didymus, and Nathanael, who was of Cana of Galilee, and the sons of Zebedee and two others of his disciples.

3. Simon Peter saith to them: I go a fishing. They say to him: We also come with thee. And they went forth and entered into the ship: and that night they caught nothing.

4. But when the morning was come, Jesus stood on the shore: yet the disciples knew not that it was Jesus.

5. Jesus therefore said to them: Children, have you any meat? They answered him: No.

6. He saith to them: Cast the net on the right side of the ship; and you shall find. They cast therefore: and now they were not able to draw it, for the multitude of fishes.

1, 2. Since St John nowhere else speaks of the 'sons of Zebedee', it is possible that these words were a marginal note explaining who the two anonymous disciples were. We learn here that Nathanael was from Cana, which fits in well with 1: 45–51 and 2: 1 ff.

3. 'To take' (πιάζειν) (fish) is not found in the Synoptists, but has occurred six times in John.

4. Since (verse 8) they were about 100 yards distant, non-recognition might be natural: but see below.

5, 6. 'Children': but the Greek (παιδία) is less intimate than τεκνία. It is more like 'You men!' because it has a slight touch of authority. 'Meat' (προσφάγιον) here means fish.

7. That disciple therefore whom Jesus loved said to Peter: It is the Lord. Simon Peter, when he heard that it was the Lord, girt his coat about him (for he was naked) and cast himself into the sea.

8. But the other disciples came in the ship (for they were not far from the land, but as it were two hundred cubits) dragging the net with fishes.

9. As soon then as they came to land, they saw hot coals lying, and a fish laid thereon, and bread.

10. Jesus saith to them: Bring hither of the fishes which you have now caught.

---

7. The episode of St Peter's swimming to shore can hardly be understood without reference to the Greek: else it is impossible to form an exact picture of what he did. St John recognizes by instinct that this must be the Lord: St Peter too, more impulsively, cannot wait to be rowed back slowly, by a boat hauling such a heavy load, but jumps into the water and swims to shore. Now 'coat' (ἐπενδύτης) certainly means an 'over-dress': on the one hand, both in Greek and Latin, γυμνός and *nudus* often mean 'wearing an under-tunic only', and on the other, Peter could hardly have swum with the voluminous oriental cloak on the top of his tunic; besides, διεζώσατο *can* mean only 'girded himself' (διεζωμένη τὴν ἐσθῆτα: 'having tied a girdle round her dress'; Lucian): so probably ἐπενδύτης means a sort of smock that he wore while fishing instead of his normal long tunic, and he bound this round his waist with e.g. a cord that lay handy: if the boat was 100 yards out, we cannot suppose that the water was still so shallow that he merely waded, not swam, and in fact the water is said to become rapidly deep. The other disciples rowed in with difficulty, if only because the fish would not have been swimming free in the great net, but have been crowded in a solid mass at the end of it.

9. One cannot tell if the Greek means 'fish and bread' or *a* fish and a loaf. Our Lord had prepared a small meal so that they could start at once:

10. but he tells them to add some of their own fish.

11. Simon Peter went up and drew the net to land, full of great fishes, one-hundred and fifty-three. And although there were so many, the net was not broken.

12. Jesus saith to them: Come and dine. And none of them who were at meat, durst ask him: Who art thou? Knowing that it was the Lord.

13. And Jesus cometh and taketh bread and giveth them: and fish in like manner.

14. This is now the third time that Jesus was manifested to his disciples, after he was risen from the dead.

---

11. Peter 'goes up' into the boat, now close to shore but with the net still attached to it. John characteristically adds the number of the fish, but also, that the net was not broken.

12, 13. Verse 12 may suggest that the intercourse between our Lord and His disciples was, after His resurrection, at least partly different from what it had been before. He gives them natural food, but seems not to have eaten (on this occasion) with them: on their side, they 'dared' not ask Him who He was, because they 'knew' it was He. Why, if they knew, would they have had to ask? Was our Lord making a sort of *transition* from the old association to the days when His bodily presence would be totally withdrawn? We may say that St John *never* relates a material event without seeing in it, or pointing by means of it towards, some spiritual doctrine. The miraculous draught of fishes told of in Luke 5: 4–11 is pure 'history', but our Lord uses it to foretell the destiny of the fishermen–disciples ('fishers of men'). Here St John tells of the net that contains the miraculous draught and is *not* broken: the contrast is obviously deliberate. Yet the story is not an 'allegory': the details about St Peter's dress, the number of the fish, correspond to nothing spiritual: but we think it significant that while all the disciples join in catching the fish, the initiative is St Peter's, and it is St Peter who personally draws the catch to shore. St John cuts the story short as he did that of Nicodemus. He does not say 'what

CHAPTER TWENTY-ONE

The Mandate given to Peter: 15–19

15. When therefore they had dined, Jesus saith to Simon Peter: Simon, *son* of John, lovest thou me more than these? He saith to him: Yea, Lord, thou knowest that I love thee. He saith to him: Feed my lambs.

16. He saith to him again: Simon, *son* of John, lovest thou me? He saith to him: Yea, Lord, thou knowest that I love thee. He saith to him: Feed my lambs.

17. He said to him the third time: Simon, son of John, lovest thou me? Peter was grieved, because he had said to him the third time: Lovest thou me? And he said to him: Lord, thou knowest all things: thou knowest that I love thee. He said to him: Feed my sheep.

---

happened next': the lesson has been sufficiently taught, especially in view of the following episode. This is the 'third' apparition, i.e. to the apostles collectively. The women had not the special apostolic vocation.

15–17. 'Eaten'; not 'dined'; this was the first meal of the day. Before the Passion, Peter had put himself forward as more loyal than the others (Matt. 26: 33; Mark 14: 29): it is to this that our Lord looks back rather than the triple denial, especially as He is about to set Peter in fact ahead of the rest. In the Greek, our Lord, in His first two questions uses a different word for 'love' from that which St Peter uses (ἀγαπᾶν and φιλεῖν): in His third question, our Lord uses St Peter's word: but it is doubtful if there is a difference in meaning between the two words. Again, our Lord says 'Feed (βόσκε) My lambs'; then, 'Shepherd (ποίμαινε), my sheep' and then returns to 'feed'. But again, we doubt if there is a real difference in the meaning. St Peter's ναί, 'yea', is not precisely an affirmation—*Yes!* It is almost a deprecation—'Surely, Lord—' but a humble one, almost as though he said: 'Dear Lord—you *know* I love you!'

We cannot but quote St Augustine: 'Hunc invenit exitum ille negator, et amator: praesumendo elatus, negando prostratus, flendo purgatus, confitendo probatus, patiendo

165

18. Amen, amen, I say to thee, when thou wast younger, thou didst gird thyself and didst walk where thou wouldst. But when thou shalt be old, thou shalt stretch forth thy hands, and another shall gird thee and lead thee whither thou wouldst not.

19. And this he said, signifying by what death he should glorify God. And when he had said this, he saith to him: Follow me.

The Destiny of John: 20–23

20. Peter turning about, saw that disciple whom Jesus loved following, who also leaned on his breast at supper and said: Lord, who is he that shall betray thee?

21. Him therefore when Peter had seen, he saith to Jesus: Lord, and what *shall* this man *do*?

22. Jesus saith to him : So I will have him to remain till I come, what is it to thee? Follow thou me.

23. This saying therefore went abroad among the brethren, that that disciple should not die. And Jesus did not say to him: He should not die; but: So I will have him to remain till I come, what is it to thee?

---

coronatus. . . . Hoc enim oportebat, ut prius Christus pro Petri salute, deinde Petrus pro Christi praedicatione moreretur.'

18, 19. The prophecy was obscure, and John needed to state its bearing definitely. Our Lord contrasts the independence and self-sufficiency of youth and the helplessness of old age. But Peter certainly understood the words to imply his death; and possibly in the words 'follow Me' heard the echo of those preceding words: 'Take up thy cross.'

20. 'Following': perhaps our Lord had taken Peter aside during the above words, and St John now approached. The evangelist leaves us in no doubt from whom this information comes.

21, 22. St Peter and St John are going to be closely associated (Acts, *passim*). St Peter says: 'And this man—what?' Our Lord gently replies: 'Suppose I should wish him to remain where he is—till I come . . . that is not *your* affair! Do *you* follow Me!' 'Till I come' undoubtedly means 'till our Lord's coming at the end of the world'.

Conclusion: 24, 25

24. This is that disciple who giveth testimony of these things and hath written these things: and we know that his testimony is true.

25. But there are also many other things which Jesus did: which, if they were written every one, the world itself, I think, would not be able to contain the books that should be written.

---

23. Who wrote this? Some think, the 'brethren', after John *had* died, so that our Lord—had He meant that John would not dic—would have made a false prediction. Others more probably hold that John simply relates what our Lord said, and leaves it without comment, save that He did *not* say that the Parousia would occur within John's lifetime.

24. It is possible that this was written by St John, but, others think, by his associates—St John *wrote* the book; that work is over: but he is still giving witness (present participle), either as surviving but writing no more; or, in the actual pages of the book. If, however, these verses are not by St John, he would seem to have left his document without adequate finish.

25. This verse, we think, must have been written by the actual scribe, if only by the unexpected οἶμαι, '*I think. . . .*' St John never speaks in the first person singular, save about his *writing*, cf. on 1: 14. The expression: 'The world . . . etc.' seems to us more rhetorical than John's way of writing: It can however be paralleled from e.g. the Jew Philo.

St John's 'Gospel' is unique in literature. It is not to take a worldly view of it if we mention his sheer power of telling a story, like that of the man born blind, the paralytic by the sheep-pool, told so rapidly and with such keen irony; his gift of conjuring up a picture in a few phrases, like that of the aged Nicodemus, or of the Samaritan woman by the well; the *music* of his Greek which enables us to catch the rhythmic, even strophaic form in which our Lord must often have spoken—especially in the Discourse on the Bread of Life. But St John begins his writing almost as if the veils of heaven were parted and as if we were to contemplate the 'inaccessible Light' in which the Eternal God and His Son are dwelling. But forthwith we are told that this vision is not yet for us: God utters His Word human-wise and He spreads His tent amongst us, Man amidst men. And John the Baptist appears as the first Witness to Him, the Baptist, summing up in himself all the prophetic history of the Old Testament, almost terrifying in his austerity till we see his perfect glad unselfishness; he steps back from the place to be held only by the one Bridegroom of the soul; his Voice is silenced and he awaits only the dungeon and the axe.

St John opens his Gospel by looking back to the book of *Genesis*—'In the beginning', and says there is to be a New Creation, a New World. The first miracle—the changing of the water into wine—teaches that our Lord is to give us something as far better than the older Revelation as wine is than water: then, He declares that this 'something' is far better than the Temple itself and all it stood for—namely, Himself. Then He goes on to explain what this gift of Himself can mean, and *how* we are to become 'new men', and that this means more than a mere improvement in our moral life (though it should include that). In the talk with Nicodemus, He remembers *Genesis* again, and how the Spirit of God set the dark lifeless waters astir and caused life to exist and then speaks of the New Birth 'by water and the Spirit' which we need if we are to be 'new men'. Then, talking with the Samaritaness, He teaches that we are not merely to be 'born anew', but to go on living a new life, the life of 'supernatural grace', as we say; the Life keeps springing up in ourselves like a source or fountain—it is not 'dead water', like what lies in a cistern. But life needs nourishment: the body needs food and drink; the mind needs intellectual education; but the supernatural life can be nourished only by God Himself, and so, after the miracle of the multiplication of bread, St John records the discourse on the Bread of Life—that Bread which is no mere memory of Christ, nor symbol of Him, but Himself, whom we receive in Holy Communion.

These are great mysteries, and we feel that they are 'too high' for us. But another main theme of this Gospel is 'Light'. 'I am the Light of the World', Jesus says (8: 12): 'I came, a Light, into the world' (12: 46), so that it is impossible that we should not see enough, if but we want to see! If we ask Him, sufficient light will be given to us—only, we must *walk* in the light; else, we should be mere wanderers, not knowing whither we are going (12: 35, 36). We have to make a choice and adhere to our Lord, else we are 'judged', in a state of separation, and there is no need for condemnation to be pronounced; just as if we do 'come to' Christ and 'hear' Him, we have 'passed from death into life': Eternal Life already exists within us (5: 22–24).

Thus in His teaching our Lord neglects no element that normal life makes use of—air, water, bread, wine; all is consecrated by Him: and again, as truly as the Synoptists do, He takes hold of that earlier revelation, the 'Old Testament', and sees that it all of it witnesses to Him who is its 'fulfilment'. But how is it that He does this? First, not anything in the world, not all the Law and the Prophets, could *give Life*. But that is what He can and does: 'Whom He will, them maketh He alive' (5: 21): and how so? Because 'even as the Father hath Life in Himself, so to the Son, too, hath He given to have Life in Himself' (5: 26). But before the great miracle of raising Lazarus from the dead, He declares—

I AM
The Resurrection and the Life.
He who believeth in Me, though he die,
Shall live;
And all who live, and believe in Me
Shall never die.
(11: 25, 26).

Thus He makes it plain that He is not only equal to God (5: 18, etc.), but *God,* and those who do not know the Son cannot claim that they know the Father (8: 19; 14: 10); and though the Father is greater than that Human Nature which is to 'fall into the earth and die' (12: 24), yet the Son and the Father are '*one thing*' (10: 38; 14: 20): 'Before Abraham came into being, I AM' (8: 58): 'he who hath seen Me, hath seen the Father' (14: 9; 12: 45).

If, after all, we still feel not only that these things are too high for us, but that the story of our Lord, as related by St John, has somehow been injured by the noise and wrangling, the jealousies and finally the murderous plotting of His enemies, when we pass into the Supper Room all this is hushed: our Lord stoops as low as any of us when He washes His disciples' feet and we realize that from first to last Love has been the explanation of that story: 'God so *loved* the world that He sent into it His Sole-Begotten Son',—into a world that was still sinful and unredeemed. All that St John has recorded in the first twelve chapters of his gospel is gathered together here; and the *mind* of Jesus Christ throughout has been what is revealed to us in His own great Prayer which fills the seventeenth chapter.

NOTE. Anyone who studies the 'Gospel according to St John' would be wise to read also his First Epistle. Light will shine from each upon the other.

APPENDIX

The Logos

It is necessary to describe briefly the background of the expression used by St John in his Prologue—the *Logos*, or Word of God. 'Word' is a poor translation of that expression, but we have none better. 'Logos' meant the *reasonable account* that could be given of something, and so, it could mean either a thought in the mind, a word on the lips or the expression of the 'idea' in a 'work of art'. Thus Newman wrote his *Idea of a University*, and an artist could say, pointing to his sculpture or painting: 'You see my idea!'. Greek philosophy, about 600 B.C., began by trying to express the whole universe in a single formula: e.g. the immanent, ultimate Fact was 'Water', or 'Fire'; that was the 'rational account' that could be given of things—their 'Logos'. In the Graeco-Roman world the idea was worked out most fully by the Stoics. The Universe was so indwelt by God as to be His adequate Logos, or self-expression, while He, in it, is *its* Logos, or explanation. Therefore the Stoic could speak of God, the Ultimate Fact: God, as containing the Universe in Himself, in His mind: and God, as expressed outwardly in the Universe. Most ancient religions described some sort of 'intermediary' between God and Creation, but here we need think only of the Alexandrian Jews who tried to express their religion in terms which would make it more acceptable to Greek thinkers. Thus Philo (d. about A.D. 50) used the 'logos' expression very freely, but not at all as St John did. In Philo, the Word is God's thought, His First-Begotten, the World being His Second-Begotten. In John, the Logos is on the whole God's 'uttered' word, and His Sole-Begotten: in

Philo the Logos is an intermediate nature, a link between God and Matter; in John, It 'mediates' because It took up human nature and joined it to Its divine nature and appeared amongst us as one Person, true God and true man, a 'fact of history'. However interestingly those other theories might wrap up their doctrine in allegory or myth, they never could assert that the Logos 'became *man*'.

John, then, does not borrow anything from pagan doctrine, though he uses a current expression. He does not say: 'Your doctrine is practically the same as mine; we mean almost the same thing.' He simply takes the term 'Logos' and declares *his* doctrine—that the Word is co-eternal with God; one with, yet mysteriously other than, the Father; that through Him the world was made, that into it He came, Light and Truth, and since for our sake He became Man, those who welcome Him are enabled to become, by no mere metaphor, children of God.[1]

---

[1] Another theory, eastern in origin, was powerful in the Graeco-Roman world, i.e. that there were *two* Ultimates, Spirit and Matter, Light and Dark, Truth and Illusion, in conflict with one another, Matter being *bad*. John certainly uses these great contrasts, but nowhere would he admit that the world was not God's creation; it was good, despite the evil that free perverted choices, angelic and human, have put into it.

QUESTIONS

1. In what sense is it true to say that the teaching of Christ as given in St John's gospel is summed up in the prologue (1: 1–14)?
2. What does this gospel tell us about St John the Baptist?
3. Narrate the call of the Apostles as given in this gospel.
4. Give an account of Our Lord's meeting with Nicodemus.
5. Give an account of the meeting with the woman of Samaria.
6. Narrate the events of the day on which Our Lord fed the five thousand and of the night following.
7. Give some explanation of Our Lord's teaching in the synagogue in Capharnaum about the bread of life.
8. Give an account of the happenings at the Feast of Tabernacles.
9. Relate the story of the cure of the man born blind.
10. Explain the parable of the Good Shepherd.
11. What does St John say about Martha and Mary of Bethany, and what is the significance of the events with which they are associated?
12. Give an account of the raising of Lazarus. What were its consequences?
13. Would you gather from St John that the Last Supper was a Paschal Supper?
14. Give some account of Our Lord's discourse and prayer at the Last Supper.
15. Describe the Passion from the arrest of Our Lord to the Scourging.
16. Describe the events of the Passion from the Crowning with Thorns to the Burial of Our Lord.

17. Give an account of the appearances of Our Lord after the Resurrection, as recorded by St John.

18. Explain the events of Our Lord's appearance by the Lake of Tiberias.

19. How can it be shown from this gospel that Christ claimed to be God, and how did He prove His claim?

20. 'But these are written that you may believe that Jesus is the Christ, the son of God; and that believing you may have life in his name.' (John 20: 31) What does St John mean here by 'life'? And show how he describes this 'life' during the course of his gospel.

21. Mention the principal points in the Fourth Gospel that are not found in the Synoptics.

22. What are the principal discourses of Christ in the Fourth Gospel?

23. Mention the miracles of Our Lord which St John describes. What is their significance?

24. What Jewish feasts are referred to in this gospel? Show briefly what connection they have with the gospel narrative.

25. What does this gospel tell us about St Peter? or about St John the Evangelist himself?

26. Are there any indications that this gospel was written by an eyewitness?

27. What is Our Lord's teaching in this gospel about 'the world'?

28. Give some account of Our Lord's instructions to the Apostles about their mission.

29. What is Our Lord's teaching about the Paraclete?

30. Give some account of Our Lord's relations with those who were hostile to Him.

31. What indications are there that St John's gospel was written some time after the other gospels?

32. 'It is to St John that we turn for portraits of individuals.' Comment on this statement.

33. Do you know of any ways in which modern archaeology has confirmed the historical accuracy of St. John's gospel?

34. Write notes on: The Feast of Tabernacles, Cephas, Bethsaida, Cana, Nicodemus, Sichar, Jacob's Well, Probatica, Siloe, Feast of Dedication, Solomon's porch, Bethania, Ephrem, Pharisees, Cedron, 'the high priest of that year', Annas, Caiaphas, Lithostrotos, Mary of Cleophas, Mary Magdalen, Joseph of Arimathea.